BARON VON STEUBEN'S

REVOLUTIONARY WAR
DRILL MANUAL

———

BARON VON STEUBEN'S

REVOLUTIONARY WAR
DRILL MANUAL

A FACSIMILE REPRINT OF THE
1794 EDITION

FREDERICK WILLIAM
BARON VON STEUBEN

DOVER PUBLICATIONS, INC.
New York

Published in Canada by General Publishing Company, Ltd., 30 Lesmill Road, Don Mills, Toronto, Ontario.
Published in the United Kingdom by Constable and Company, Ltd.

This Dover edition, first published in 1985, is an unabridged republication of *Regulations for the Order and Discipline of the Troops of the United States. To Which Is Added, An Appendix, Containing, the United States Militia Act, Passed in Congress, May, 1792,* published by I[saiah] Thomas and E[benezer] T. Andrews, Boston, in 1794 (with the title page showing the author's name as Baron de Stuben) as a "new edition" of the regulations approved by Congress on March 29, 1779. For the Dover edition, a new Publisher's Note has been prepared and foldout plates have been converted to single- or double-page plates.

The publisher is grateful to The Corning Museum of Glass for making the 1794 edition available for reproduction.

Manufactured in the United States of America
Dover Publications, Inc., 31 East 2nd Street, Mineola, N.Y. 11501

Library of Congress Cataloging in Publication Data

United States. War Dept. Inspector General's Office.
Baron von Steuben's Revolutionary War drill manual.

Reprint: Originally published: Regulations for the order and discipline of the troops of the United States to which is added an appendix containing the United States Militia Act, passed in Congress, May 1792. Boston : I. Thomas and E. T. Andrews, 1794.
    1. Military law—United States. 2. United States. Army—Regulations. 3. United States. Army. Infantry—Drill manuals. I. Steuben, Friedrich Wilhelm Ludolf Gerhard Augustin, Baron von, 1730–1794. II. United States. Militia Act. III. Title. IV. Title: Revolutionary War drill manual.
KF7305.A33 1985   343.73'01   85-10266
ISBN 0-486-24934-4 (pbk.) 347.3031

PUBLISHER'S NOTE

Baron von Steuben, who played a crucial role in the
military success of the American Revolution, was born
Friedrich Wilhelm Ludolf Gerhard Augustin von
Steuben on September 17, 1730, in Magdeburg, Prus-
sia, to a military family. In America he was known as
Frederick William Augustus von (or de) Steuben.

Entering the officer corps of the Prussian army at the
age of sixteen, Steuben served until the end of the
Seven Years' War (1756–63), rising to the rank of captain. For a time he was attached to the general staff of
Frederick the Great. Leaving the army shortly after the
Peace of Hubertusburg in 1763, Steuben at some unre-
corded date during the next twelve years appears to
have been created a baron (*Freiherr*), while acting as
court chamberlain to the Prince of Hohenzollern-
Hechingen. Yet he left Hohenzollern-Hechingen under
obscure circumstances, and deeply in debt, in 1775 to
seek posts with the British East India Company and the
French and Prussian armies. All of these efforts came
to nothing. At last, in the summer of 1777 he was
brought to the attention of Benjamin Franklin, then in
Paris as an agent of the embattled British colonies. By
letter, Franklin presented him to George Washington as
"a Lieutenant General in the King of Prussia's service,"
a vastly imposing, if fictitious, rank that greatly im-
pressed both Washington and the Continental Congress—as did Steuben's offer to accept only his ex-
penses as payment until the Revolutionary cause
succeeded. He was directed to report to General Wash-

ington at the Continental Army's bleak winter encampment at Valley Forge in February 1778.

With his striking combination of qualities rare among the insurgents—his high professional military reputation, forceful Prussian bearing, and colorful personality—Steuben had a galvanizing effect on the downhearted, disorganized army and immediately became one of Washington's most valued and trusted officers, winning appointment as inspector general and a mandate to train the army as an efficient fighting machine. All this despite the fact that Steuben spoke virtually no English and was obliged to work through interpreters.

At Valley Forge, Steuben formed a model drill company of one hundred specially selected men and undertook to drill them in person. As the drills progressed, he began to write (in brief installments, in French) the drill instructions that grew into the *Regulations for the Order and Discipline of the Troops of the United States.* This manual of drill and field-service regulations became the foundation of military training and procedure. Commonly known as the army's "blue book," and considered only slightly less authoritative than the Bible, it remained the official United States military guide until 1812.

Steuben's transformation of his model company into a precision unit captured the imagination of the entire army. Rigorous drill suddenly caught on with the troops and led to what has been called "perhaps the most remarkable achievement in rapid military training in the history of the world." By spring, Washington had acknowledged Steuben's achievement by raising him to the rank of major general. From this turning point until the end of the war, the improvised Continental Army maintained a level of discipline comparable to that of the British regulars, with their centuries-old tradition.

In 1780, Washington granted Steuben's wish for a command. He served as a division commander in the final siege of Yorktown, where his intimate experience with siege tactics in the Seven Years' War contributed substantially to the final defeat of the British. Washington's last official act as wartime commander was to write a letter to Steuben commending his service.

After the coming of peace, Steuben became an American citizen, retired from the army, and made his home in New York. In 1786 the state of New York granted him 16,000 acres north of what is now Utica. As in his youth, however, Steuben was improvident about personal finances; a group of influential friends, Alexander Hamilton among them, had to rescue him from bankruptcy in 1790, the same year that the federal government finally decided to repay his wartime service with an annual pension of $2,500. He died on November 28, 1794.

Baron von Steuben brought unique qualities to the Revolutionary cause: his depth of military training and minutely detailed grasp of the techniques of command were precisely what the bedraggled Continental Army desperately needed. He was among the few truly indispensable figures in the achievement of independence. His likeness can be seen in John Trumbull's mural *The Surrender of Lord Cornwallis at Yorktown* in the rotunda of the Capitol, in Washington, D.C.

Baron von Steuben's regulations were officially approved by Congress on March 29, 1779. This Dover facsimile reproduces the "*new* EDITION, illustrated

by eight COPPERPLATES, accurately engraved . . .
PRINTED AT *BOSTON*, BY I. THOMAS AND E. T.
ANDREWS" in 1794. (The firm of Thomas & Andrews was comprised of the renowned printer and historian of the press Isaiah Thomas—the leading publisher of his day—whose premises were established in Worcester, Massachusetts, and his Boston partner, Ebenezer T. Andrews.) As in the 1794 edition, in the present volume the Table of Contents appears on pages 153–155, followed by the Explanation of the Plates and the Appendix (the United States Militia Act of 1792).

BARON VON STEUBEN'S
REVOLUTIONARY WAR
DRILL MANUAL

———

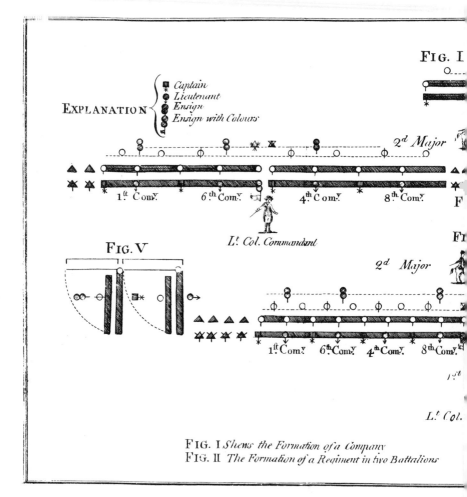

Fig. I

2ᵈ Major

1ˢᵗ Comʸ.   6ᵗʰ Comʸ.   4ᵗʰ Comʸ.   8ᵗʰ Comʸ.   F

Lᵗ Col. Commandant

Fig. V

2ᵈ Major

Fᴵ

1ˢᵗ Comʸ.   6ᵗʰ Comʸ.   4ᵗʰ Comʸ.   8ᵗʰ Comʸ.

Lᵗ Col.

FIG. I *Shews the Formation of a Company*
FIG. II *The Formation of a Regiment in two Battalions*

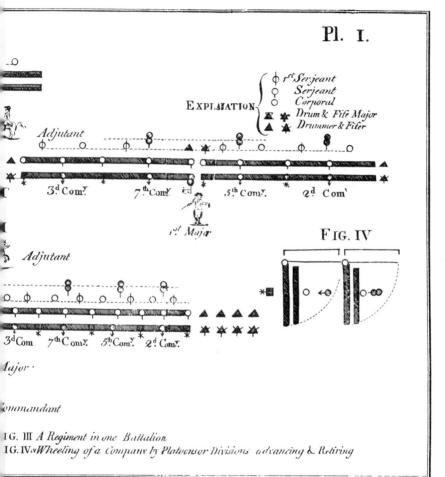

Pl. I.

EXPLANATION
- φ 1st Serjeant
- Serjeant
- ○ Corporal
- ✗ ✸ Drum & Fife Major
- ▲ ▲ Drummer & Fifer

Adjutant

3^d Com^y. 7th Com^y. 5th Com^y. 2^d Com^y.

1st Major

FIG. IV

Adjutant

3^d Com 7th Com^y. 5th Com^y. 2^d Com^y.

Major

Commandant

IG. III *A Regiment in one Battalion*
IG. IV. *Wheeling of a Company by Platoons or Divisions advancing & Retiring*

Doolittle sc.

REGULATIONS

FOR THE

ORDER AND DISCIPLINE

OF THE

TROOPS OF THE UNITED STATES.

TO WHICH IS ADDED,

AN APPENDIX,

CONTAINING, THE

UNITED STATES MILITIA ACT,

PASSED IN CONGRESS, MAY, 1792.

A *new* EDITION, illuftrated by eight COPPERPLATES, accurately
engraved.

By BARON DE STUBEN,
Late MAJOR GENERAL and INSPECTOR GENERAL of the ARMY of
the UNITED STATES.

PRINTED AT *BOSTON*,
BY I. THOMAS AND E. T. ANDREWS,
FAUST's STATUE, No. 45, NEWBURY STREET.

1794.

In CONGRESS, 29th March, 1779.

CONGRESS *judging it of the greateſt importance to preſcribe ſome invariable rules
for the order and diſcipline of the troops, eſpeci-
ally for the purpoſe of introducing an uniformity
in their formation and manoeuvres, and in the
ſervice of the camp :*

ORDERED, *That the following regulations
be obſerved by all the troops of the United
States, and that all general and other officers
cauſe the ſame to be executed with all poſſible
exactneſs.*

By Order,

JOHN JAY, PRESIDENT.

Atteſt.

CHARLES THOMPSON,

Secretary.

A 2

REGULATIONS, &c.

CHAPTER I.

Of the Arms and Accoutrements of the Officers,
Non-commiſſioned Officers, and Soldiers.

THE arms and accoutrements of the officers, non-commiſſioned officers, and ſoldiers, ſhould be uniform throughout.

The officers who exerciſe their functions on horſeback, are to be armed with ſwords, the platoon officers with ſwords and eſpontoons, the non-commiſſioned officers with ſwords, fire-locks, and bayonets, and the ſoldiers with fire-locks and bayonets.

CHAPTER

CHAPTER II.

Objects with which the Officers and Non-commiſſioned Officers ſhould be acquainted.

THE officers and non-commiſſioned officers of each regiment, are to be perfectly acquainted with the manual exercife, marchings and firings, that they may be able to inftruct their foldiers when neceſſary ; they muft alſo be acquainted with the drefs, difcipline, and police of the troops, and with every thing that relates to the fervice.

The commanding officer of each regiment is to be anſwerable for the general inftruction of the regiment, and is to exercife, or caufe to be exercifed, the officers, non-commiſſioned officers, and foldiers, whenever he thinks proper.

CHAPTER III.

Of the Formation of a Company.

(Plate I. Figure 1.)

A COMPANY is to be formed in two ranks, at one pace diftance, with the talleft men in the rear, and both ranks fized, with the
ſhorteft

ſhorteſt men of each in the centre. A company thus drawn up is to be divided into two
ſections or platoons ; the captain to take poſt
on the right of the firſt platoon, covered by a
ſerjeant ; the lieutenant on the right of the
ſecond platoon, alſo covered by a ſerjeant ; the
enſign four paces behind the centre of the company ; the firſt ſerjeant two paces behind the
centre of the firſt platoon, and the eldeſt corporal two paces behind the ſecond platoon ; the
other two corporals are to be on the flanks of
the front rank.

C H A P T E R IV.
Of the Formation of a Regiment.
(Plat I. Figure 2 and 3.)

A REGIMENT is to conſiſt of eight companies, which are to be poſted in the following order, from right to left.

First captain's.
Colonel's.
Fourth captain's.
Major's.
Third captain's.
Lieutenant colonel's.
Fifth captain's.
Second captain's.

For

For the greater facility in manœuvring, each regiment confisting of more than one hundred and fixty files, is to be formed in two battalions, (fig. 2.) with an interval of twenty paces between them, and one colour posted in the centre of each battalion ; the colonel fifteen paces before the centre of the firft battalion ; the lieutenant-colonel fifteen paces before the centre of the fecond battalion ; the major fifteen paces behind the interval of the two battalions ; the adjutant two paces from the major ; the drum and fife-major two paces behind the centre of the firft battalion ; their places behind the fecond battalion being fupplied by a drum and fife ; and the other drums and fifes equally divided on the wings of each battalion.

When a regiment is reduced to one hundred and fixty files, it is to be formed in one battalion, with both colours in the centre ; the colonel fixteen paces before the colours; the lieutenant colonel eight paces behind the colonel ; the major fifteen paces behind the centre of the battalion, having the adjutant at his fide ; the drum and fife major two paces behind the centre of the battalion ; and the drums and fifes equally divided on the wings.

Every

Every battalion, whether it compofe the whole, or only half of a regiment, is to be divided into four divifions and eight platoons ; no platoon to confift of lefs than ten files ; fo that a regiment confifting of lefs than eighty files, cannot form a battalion, but muft be incorporated with fome other, or employed on detachment.

In cafe of the abfence of any field officer, his place is to be filled by the officer next in rank in the regiment ; and in order that the officers may remain with their refpective companies, if any company officer is abfent, his place fhall be fupplied by the officer next in rank in the fame company ; but fhould it happen that a company is left without an officer, the colonel or commanding officer may order an officer of another company to take the command, as well for the exercife as for the difcipline and police of the company in camp.

When the light company is with the regiment it muft be formed twenty paces on the right on the parade, but muft not interfere with the exercife of the battalion, but exercife by itfelf ; and when the light infantry are embodied, every four companies will form a battalion

talion, and exercise in the fame manner as the battalion in the line.

CHAPTER V.
Of the Inſtruction of Recruits.

THE commanding officer of each company is charged with the inſtruction of his recruits; and as that is a ſervice that requires not only experience, but a patience and temper not met with in every officer, he is to make choice of an officer, ſerjeant, and one or two corporals of his company, who, being approved of by the colonel, are to attend particularly to that buſineſs : but in caſe of the arrival of a great number of recruits, every officer without diſtinction is to be employed on that ſervice.

The commanding officer of each regiment will fix on ſome place for the exerciſe of his recruits, where himſelf or ſome field-officer muſt attend, to overlook their inſtruction.

The recruits muſt be taken ſingly, and firſt taught to put on their accoutrements, and carry themſelves properly.

The Poſition of a Soldier without Arms.
He is to ſtand ſtraight and firm upon his
legs,

legs, with the head turned to the right fo far as to bring the left eye over the waiftcoat buttons; the heels two inches apart; the toes turned out; the belly drawn in a little, but without conftraint; the breaft a little projected; the fhoulders fquare to the front, and kept back; and the hands hanging down the fides, with the palms clofe to the thighs.

Attention !

At this word the foldier muft be filent, ftand firm and fteady, moving neither hand nor foot, (except as ordered) but attend carefully to the words of command.

This attention of the foldier muft be obferved in the ftricteft manner, till he receives the word

Reft !

At which he may refrefh himfelf, by moving his hands or feet; but muft not then fit down or quit his place, unlefs permitted fo to do.

Attention !

To the Left,—Drefs !

At this word the foldier turns his head brifkly to the left, fo as to bring his right eye in the direction of his waiftcoat buttons.

To

To the Right——Drefs !

The foldier dreffes again to the right, as before.

The recruit muft then be taught

The Facings.

To the Right,——Face ! Two motions.

1ft. Turn brifkly on both heels to the right, lifting up the toes a little, and defcribing the quarter of a circle.

2d. Bring back the right foot to its proper pofition, without ftamping.

To the Left,——Face ! Two motions.

1ft. Turn to the left as before to the right.

2d. Bring up the right foot to its proper pofition.

To the Right about,—Face ! Three motions.

1ft. Step back with the right foot, bringing the buckle oppofite the left heel, at the fame time feizing the cartridge-box with the right hand.

2d. Turn brifkly on both heels, and defcribe half a circle.

3d. Bring back the right foot, at the fame time quitting the cartridge-box.

When

When the recruit is fufficiently expert in the foregoing points, he muft be taught the different fteps.

The Common Step

Is two feet, and about feventy-five in a mi. nute.

To the Front,——March !

The foldier fteps off with his left foot, and marches a free, eafy and natural ftep, without altering the pofition of his body or head, taking care to preferve a proper balance, and not crofs his legs, but to march without conftraint in every fort of ground : The officer muft march fometimes in his front and fometimes at his fide, in order to join example to precept.

Halt !

At this word the foldier ftops fhort, on the foot then advanced, immediately bringing up the other, without ftamping.

The Quick Step

Is alfo two feet, but about one hundred and twenty in a minute, and is performed on the fame principle as the other.

B

The

The recruits having been exercifed fingly, till they have a proper carriage, and are well grounded in the different fteps ; the officer will then take three men, and placing them in one rank, exercife them in the different fteps, and teach them

The March by Files,

Which, being of great importance, muft be carefully attended to ; obferving that the foldier carries his body more forward than in the front march, and that he does not increafe the diftance from his file-leader.

The Oblique Step

Muft then be practifed, both in the quick and common time.

In marching obliquely to the right, the foldier fteps obliquely with the right foot, bringing up the left, and placing the heel directly before the toes of the right foot, and the contrary when marching to the left ; at the fame time obferving to keep the fhoulders fquare to the front, efpecially that the fhoulder oppofed to the fide they march to does not project, and that the files keep clofe.

The

The recruits being thus far inftructed, muft be again taken feparately, and taught

The Pofition of a Soldier under Arms.

In this pofition the foldier is to ftand ftraight and firm upon his legs, with the heels two inches apart, the toes a little turned out, the belly drawn in a little without conftraint, the breaft a little projected, the fhoulders fquare to the front and kept back, the right hand hanging down the fide, with the palm clofe to the thigh, the left elbow not turned out from the body, the firelock carried on the left fhoulder, at fuch height that the guard will be juft under the left breaft, the fore-finger and thumb before the fwell of the butt, the three laft fingers under the butt, the flat of the butt againft the hip bone, and preffed fo as that the firelock may be felt againft the left fide, and ftand before the hollow of the fhoulder, neither leaning towards the head nor from it the barrel almoft perpendicular. When exercifing, he is to be very exact in counting a fecond of time between each motion.

The MANUAL EXERCISE.

I.

Poife——Firelock! Two motions.

1ft. With your left hand turn the firelock brifkly, bringing the lock to the front, at the
fame inftant feize it with the right hand
juft below the lock, keeping the piece
perpendicular.

2d. With a quick motion bring up the firelock
from the fhoulder directly before the face,
and feize it with the left hand juft above
the lock, fo that the little finger may reft
upon the feather fpring, and the thumb lie
on the ftock ; the left hand muft be of an
equal height with the eyes.

II.

Cock——Firelock ! Two motions.

1ft. Turn the barrel oppofite to your face, and
place your thumb upon the cock, raifing
the elbow fquare at this motion.

2d. Cock the firelock by drawing down your
elbow, immediately placing your thumb
upon the breech-pin, and the fingers under
the guard.

III

III.

Take Aim ! One motion.

Step back about fix inches with the right foot, bringing the left toe to the front ; at the fame time drop the muzzle, and bring up the butt-end of the firelock againſt your right fhoulder ; place the left hand forward on the fwell of the ſtock, and the fore-finger of the right hand before the trigger; finking the muzzle a little below a level, and with the right eye looking along the barrel.

IV.

Fire ! One motion.

Pull the trigger brifkly, and immediately after bringing up the right foot, come to the priming poſition, placing the heels even, with the right toe pointing to the right, the lock oppoſite the right breaſt, the muzzle directly to the front and as high as the hat, the left hand juſt forward of the feather-ſpring, holding the piece firm and ſteady ; and at the fame time feize the cock with the fore-finger and thumb of the right hand, the back of the hand turned up.

B 3   V

V.

Half-Cock ——*Firelock !* One motion.

Half bend the cock brifkly, bringing down the elbow to the butt of the firelock.

VI.

Handle——*Cartridge !* One motion.

Bring your right hand fhort round to your pouch, flapping it hard, feize the cartridge, and bring it with a quick motion to your mouth, bite the top off down to the powder, covering it inftantly with your thumb, and bring the hand as low as the chin, with the elbow down.

VII.

Prime ! One motion.

Shake the powder into the pan, and covering the cartridge again, place the three laft fingers behind the hammer, with the elbow up.

VIII.

Shut——*Pan !* Two motions.

1ft. Shut your pan brifkly, bringing down the elbow to the butt of the firelock, holding the cartridge faft in your hand.

2d. Turn the piece nimbly round before you to the loading pofition, with the lock to
the

the front, and the muzzle at the height of the chin, bringing the right hand up under the muzzle ; both feet being kept faſt in this motion.

IX.

Charge with Cartridge ! Two motions.

1ſt. Turn up your hand and put the cartridge into the muzzle, ſhaking the powder into the barrel.

2d. Turning the ſtock a little towards you, place your right hand cloſed, with a quick and ſtrong motion, upon the butt of the rammer, the thumb upwards, and the elbow down.

X.

Draw——Rammer ! Two motions.

1ſt. Draw your rammer with a quick motion half out, feizing it inſtantly at the muzzle back-handed.

2d. Draw it quite out, turn it, and enter it into the muzzle.

XI.

Ram down——Cartridge ! One motion.

Ram the cartridge well down the barrel, and inſtantly recovering and feizing the rammer back-handed

back-handed by the middle , draw it quite out,
turn it, and enter it as far as the lower pipe,
placing at the fame time the edge of the hand
on the butt-end of the rammer, with the fingers
extended.

XII.
Return——Rammer ! One motion.

Thruft the rammer home, and inftantly bring
up the piece with the left hand to the fhoulder,
feizing it at the fame time with the right hand
under the cock, keeping the left hand at the
fwell, and turning the body fquare to the front.

XIII.
Shoulder——Firelock ! Two motions.

1ft. Bring down the left hand, placing it ftrong
upon the butt.

2d. With a quick motion bring the right hand
down by your fide.

XIV.
Order——Firelock ! Two motions.

1ft. Sink the firelock with the left hand as low
as poffible, without conftraint, and at the
fame time bringing up the right hand,
feize the firelock at the left fhoulder.

2d. Quit the firelock with the left hand, and
with the right bring it down the right
fide,

fide, the butt on the ground, even with
the toes of the right foot, the thumb of
the right hand lying along the barrel, and
the muzzle being kept at a little diftance
from the body.

XV.

Ground——Firelock ! Two motions.

1ft. With the right hand turn the firelock,
bringing the lock to the rear, and inftantly ftepping forward with the left foot
a large pace, lay the piece on the ground,
the barrel in a direct line from front to
rear, placing the left hand on the knee,
to fupport the body, the head held up,
the right hand and left heel in a line, and
the right knee brought almoft to the
ground.

2d. Quitting the firelock, raife yourfelf up, and
bring back the left foot to its former
pofition.

XVI.

Take up——Firelock ! Two motions.

1ft. Step forward with the left foot, fink the
body, and come to the pofition defcribed
in the fitft motion of grounding.

2d.

2d. Raife up yourfelf and firelock, ftepping back again with the left foot, and as foon as the piece is perpendicular, turn the barrel behind, thus coming to the order.

XVII.

Shoulder——Firelock ! Two motions.

1ft. Bring the firelock to the left fhoulder, throwing it up a little, and catching it below the tail-pipe, and inftantly feize it with the left hand at the butt.

2d. With a quick motion bring the right hand down by your fide.

XVIII.

Secure——Firelock ! Three motions.

1ft. Bring up the right hand brifkly, and place it under the cock.

2d. Quit the butt with the left hand, and feize the firelock at the fwell, bringing the arm clofe down upon the lock, the right hand being kept faft in this motion, and the piece upright.

3d. Quitting the piece with your right hand, bring it down by your fide, at the fame time with your left hand throw the muzzle directly forward, bringing it within about one foot of the ground, and the butt clofe
up

up behind the left fhoulder, holding the left hand in a line with the waift belt, and with that arm covering the lock.

XIX.

Shoulder——Firelock! Three motions.

1ft. Bring the firelock up to the fhoulder, feizing it with the right hand under the cock.

2d. Bring the left hand down ftrong upon the butt.

3d. Bring the right hand down by your fide.

XX.

Fix——Bayonet! Three motions.

1ft and 2d motion the fame as the two firft motions of the fecure.

3d. Quitting the piece with your right hand, fink it with your left down the left fide, as far as may be without conftraint, at the fame time feize the bayonet with the right hand, draw and fix it, immediately flipping the hand down to the ftock, and preffing in the piece to the hollow of the fhoulder.

XXI.

Shoulder——Firelock! Three motions.

1ft. Quitting the piece with the right hand, with the left bring it up to the fhoulder, and

and feize it again with the right hand under the cock, as in the fecond motion of
the fecure.

2d. Bring the left hand down ftrong upon the
butt.

3d. Bring the right hand down by your fide.

XXII.

Prefent——Arms! Three motions.

1ft and 2d motion the fame as in coming to the
poife.

3d. Step brifkly back with your right foot,
placing it a hand's breadth diftant from
your left heel, at the fame time bring down
the firelock as quick as poffible to the reft,
finking it as far down before your left knee
as your right hand will permit without
conftraint, holding the right hand under
the guard, with the fingers extended, and
drawing in the piece with the left hand
till the barrel is perpendicular ; during this
motion you quit the piece with the left
hand, and inftantly feize it again juft below the tail-pipe.

XXIII.

Shoulder——Firelock! Two motions.

1ft. Lift up your right foot and place it by your
left

left, at the fame time bring the firelock to your left fhoulder, and feize the butt-end with the left hand, coming to the pofition of the firft motion of the fecure.

2d. Bring the right hand down by your fide.

XXIV.
Charge Bayonet !—Two motions.

1ft. The fame as the firft motion of the fecure.

2d. Bring the butt of the firelock under the right arm, letting the piece fall down ftrong on the palm of the left hand, which receives it at the fwell, the muzzle pointing directly to the front, the butt preffed with the arm againft the fide ; the front rank holding their pieces horizontally, and the rear rank the muzzles of theirs fo high as to clear the heads of the front rank, both ranks keeping their feet faft.

XXV.
Shoulder——Firelock ! Two motions.

1ft. Bring up the piece fmartly to a fhoulder, feizing the butt with the left hand.

2d. Bring the right hand down by your fide.

XXVI.
Advance—Arms ! Four motions.

1ft and 2d the fame as the two firft motions of the poife.   C   8d.

3d. Bring the firelock down to the right side, with the right hand as low as it will admit without constraint, slipping up the left hand at the same time to the swell, and instantly shifting the position of the right hand, take the guard between the thumb and forefinger, and bring the three last fingers under the cock, with the barrel to the rear.

4th. Quit the firelock with the left hand, bringing it down by your side.

XXVII.
Shoulder—Firelock ! Four motions,

1st. Bring up the left hand, and seize the firelock at the swell ; instantly shifting the right hand to its former position.

2d. Come smartly up to a poise.

3d and 4th. Shoulder.

Explanation of Priming and Loading, as performed in the Firings.

Prime and Load ! Fifteen motions.

1st. Come to the recover, throwing up your firelock, with a smart spring of the left hand, directly before the left breast, and turning the barrel inwards ; at that moment

ment catch it with the right hand below the lock, and inftantly bringing up the left hand, with a rapid motion, feize the piece clofe above the lock, the little finger touching the feather-fpring ; the left hand to be at an equal height with the eyes, the butt of the firelock clofe to the left breaft, but not preffed, and the barrel perpendicular.

2d. Bring the firelock down with a brifk motion to the *priming pofition,* as directed in in the 4th word of command, inftantly placing the thumb of the right hand againft the face of the fteel, the fingers clenched, and the elbow a little turned out, that the wrift may be clear of the cock.

3d. Open the pan by throwing back the fteel with a ftrong motion of the right arm, keeping the firelock fteady in the left hand.

4th. Handle cartridge.

5th. Prime.

6th. Shut pan.

7th. Caft about.

8th and 9th. Load.

10th and 11th. Draw rammer.

12th. Ram down cartridge.

13th. Return rammer.

14th and 15th. Shoulder.

C 2   N.B.

N. B. The motion of recover, coming down to the priming pofition, and opening the pan, to be done in the ufual time, the motions of handling the cartridge to fhutting the pan, to be done as quick as poffible ; when the pans are fhut, make a fmall paufe, and caft about together ; then the loading and fhouldering motions are to be done as quick as poffible.

Pofition of each Rank in the Firings.

Front Rank ! Make ready ! One motion.

Spring the firelock brifkly to a recover, as foon as the left hand feizes the firelock above the lock, the right elbow is to be nimbly raifed a little, placing the thumb of that hand upon the cock, the fingers open by the plate of the lock, and as quick as poffible cock the piece, by dropping the elbow, and forcing down the cock with the thumb, immediately feizing the firelock with the right hand, clofe under the lock ; the piece to be held in this manner perpendicular, oppofite the left fide of the face, the body kept ftraight, and as full to the front as poffible, and the head held up, looking well to the right.

Take Aim ! Fire !
As before explained.   *Rear*

Rear rank ! Make ready ! One motion.

Recover and cock as before directed, at the same time stepping about fix inches to the right, so as to place yourself oppofite the interval of the front rank.

Take Aim ! Fire !
As before explained.

The recruits being thus far inftructed, the officer muft take twelve men, and placing them in one rank, teach them *to drefs* to the right and left ; to do which the foldier muft obferve to feel the man on that fide he dreffes to, without crowding him, and to advance or retire, till he can juft difcover the breaft of the fecond man from him, taking care not to ftoop, but to keep his head and body upright.

When they can drefs pretty well, they muft be taught *to wheel*, as follows :

To the Right,—Wheel !
At this word of command the men turn their heads brifkly to the left, except the left hand man.

March !
The whole ftep off, obferving to feel the hand they wheel to, without crowding ; the
C 3   right

right hand man, ferving as a pivot for the reft
to turn on, gains no ground, but turns on his
heel ; the officer will march on the flank, and
when the wheeling is finifhed, command,

Halt !

On which the whole ftop fhort on the foot
then forward, bringing up the other foot, and
dreffing to the right.

To the Left,—Wheel !

The whole continue to look to the right, except the right hand man, who looks to the left.

March !

As before explained.

N. B. The wheelings muft firft be taught in
the common ftep, and then practifed in the
quick ftep.

When the recruits have practifed the foregoing exercifes, till they are fufficiently expert, they muft be fent to exercife with their
company.

CHAPTER

CHAPTER VI.

The Exercise of a Company.

ARTICLE I.

Of opening the Ranks.

Rear Rank ! Take—Diſtance !

March !

THE rear rank ſteps back four paces, and dreſſes by the right ; the officers at the ſame time advancing eight paces to the front, and dreſſing in a line ; the ſerjeants who covered the officers, take their places in the front rank ; the non-commiſſioned officers who were in the rear, remain there, ſtepping back four paces behind the rear rank.

Rear Rank ! Cloſe to the Front !

The officers face to the company.

March !

The rear rank cloſes to within a common pace, or two feet ; and the officers return to their former poſts.

ARTICLE II.

Of the Firings.

The captain will divide his company into two or more ſections, and teach them the fire by platoons, as directed in chap. XIII. art. 1,2.

The

The officers muſt give the words of command with a loud and diſtinct voice ; obſerve that the ſoldiers ſtep off, and place their feet, as directed in the manual exerciſe ; and that they level their pieces at a proper height ; for which purpoſe they muſt be accuſtomed always to take ſight at ſome object.

The officer will often command, *As you were!* to accuſtom the ſoldier not to fire till he receives the word of command.

In all exerciſes in detail, the men will uſe a piece of wood, inſtead of a flint ; and each ſoldier ſhould have ſix pieces of wood, in the form of cartridges, which the ſerjeant muſt ſee taken out of the pieces when the exerciſe is finiſhed.

When the company exerciſes with powder, the captain will inſpect the company, and ſee that all the cartridges not uſed are returned.

A r t i c l e 3.

Of the March.

In *marching to the front,* the men muſt be accuſtomed to dreſs to the centre, which they will have to do when exerciſing in battalion ;
and

and for this purpofe a ferjeant muft be placed fix paces in front of the centre, who will take fome object in front to ferve as a direction for him to march ftraight forward ; and the men muft look inwards, and regulate their march by him.

The captain muft exercife his company in different forts of ground ; and when by the badnefs of the ground, or any other accident, the foldier lofes his ftep, he muft immediately take it again from the ferjeant in the centre. The officers muft not fuffer the leaft inattention, but punifh every man guilty of it.

The Oblique March

Muft be practifed both in the quick and common ftep, agreeably to the inftructions already given.

The March by Files

Is as important as difficult. In performing it, the officers muft be attentive that the foldiers bend their bodies a little forward, and do not open their files.

The leading file will be conducted by the officer ; who will poft himfelf for that purpofe

on

on its left, when they march by the right, and the contrary when they march by the left.

The Counter March.

Note. This march muft never be executed by larger portions of a battalion than platoons.

Caution.

Take Care to counter march from the Right, by Platoons !

To the Right,—face ! March !

The whole facing to the right, each platoon wheels by files to the right about ; and when the right hand file gets on the ground where the left ftood, the officer orders,

Halt ! To the Left,—Face !

and the company will be formed with their front changed.

A R T I C L E 4.

Of Wheeling.

The captain will exercife his company in wheeling entire, and by fections or platoons, both in the common and quick ftep, taking care that the men in the rear rank incline a little

to

to the right or left, according to the hand they wheel to, fo as always to cover exactly their file-leaders.

Of Breaking off, and Forming by the oblique Step.

The captain having divided his company into two fections, will give the word,

Sections ! Break off !

Upon which the section on the right inclines by the oblique ftep to the left, and that on the left, following the former, inclines to the right, till they cover each other, when they march forward.

Form Company !

The firft section inclines to the right, fhortening its ftep, and the fecond to the left, lengthening its ftep, till they are uncovered, when both march forward, and form in a line.

Two or more companies may be joined to perform the company exercife, when they have been fufficiently exercifed by fingle companies, but

but not till then ; the inattention of the foldiers, and difficulty of inftructing them, in-
creafing in proportion with the numbers.

CHAPTER VII.

Exercife of a Battalion.

WHEN a battalion parades for exercife,
it is to be formed, and the officers pofted, agreeably to the inftructions already given
in the third and fourth chapters.

The battalion being formed, it is then to perform the manual exercife, and the wheelings,
marches, manœuvres and firings defcribed in
this and the following chapters, or fuch of
them as fhall be ordered.

N. B. When a battalion performs the firings,
the fix centre files, (viz. three on each fide the
colours,) are not to fire, but remain as a referve
for the colours ; and the officers of the two
centre platoons are to warn them accordingly.

The battalion will wheel by divifions or platoons, by word of command from the officer
commanding.   *By*

$$By \begin{cases} Platoons\ ! \\ Divifions\ ! \end{cases} To\ the \begin{cases} Right, \\ Left, \end{cases} Wheel\ !$$

March !

When the battalion wheels, the platoons are conducted by the officers commanding them ; the fupernumeraries remaining in the rear of their refpective platoons.

[See Plate I. Figure 4 and 5.]

The colours take poft between the fourth and fifth platoons

The wheeling finifhed, each officer commanding a platoon or divifion, commands

Halt ! Drefs to the Right !
and pofts himfelf before the centre, the ferjeant who covered him taking his place on the right.

Forward,—March !

The whole ftep off, and follow the leading divifion or platoon ; the officer who conducts the column receiving his directions from the commanding officer. When the battalion wheels to the right, the left flank of the platoons muft

D   drefs

drefs in a line with each other, and the contrary when they wheel to the left.

Battalion ! Halt !

By Platoons !   To the Left,—Wheel !

March !
The wheeling finifhed, each officer commanding a platoon or divifion, orders

Halt ! Drefs to the Right !
dreffes his platoon, and takes poft in the interval, the battalion being now formed in a line.

C H A P T E R   VIII.

Of the Points of View.

[Plate II. Figure 1.]
THE ufe of thefe is a moft effential part in the manœuvres, which, without them, cannot be executed with facility or precifion. They are ufually fome diftant objects, (the moft confpicuous that can be found) chofen by the commanding officer, to determine the direction of his line, which otherwife would be mere hazard.

The

The commanding officer having determined on the direction of his line, and his points of view B C, fends out two officers, D E, to feek two intermediate points in the fame line ; the officer E advances ; when D finds him in a direct line between himfelf and the point of view B, he advances, taking care to keep E always between him and the point B, which he muft do by making him fignals to advance or retire ; when E finds D in the direct line between him and C, he makes him the fignal to halt, and they will find themfelves in the intermediate points D E.

CHAPTER IX.

Of the Formation and Difplaying of Columns, with the Method of changing Front.

ARTICLE I.

The clofe Column formed on the Ground by the Right, the Right in Front.

[Plate II. Figure 2.]

D 2   Caution

Caution by the commanding officer.

Take Care to form Column by Platoons by the Right ; the Right in Front !

To the Right,—Face !

THE whole face to the right, except the right platoon ; at the same time the leading file of each platoon breaks off, in order to march in the rear of its preceding platoon.

March !

The whole step off with the quick step, each platoon marching close in the rear of that preceding it, to its place in the column.

The officers commanding platoons, when they perceive their leading file dressed with that of the platoon already formed, command

Halt ! Front ! Dress !

and the platoon fronts and dresses to the right.

A R T I C L E   2.

Display of a Column formed by the Right, the Right in Front.
[Plate II. Figure 2.]

Caution

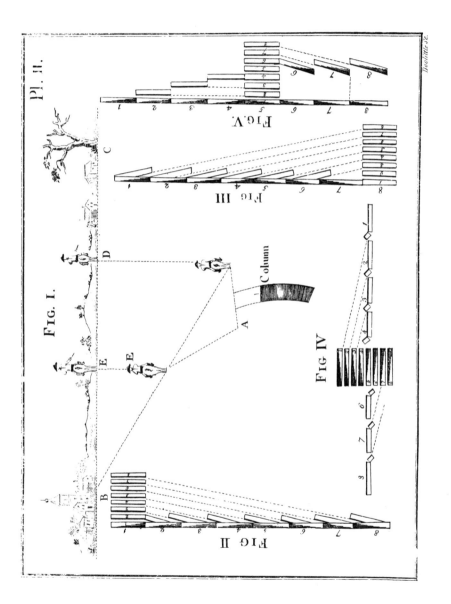

Pl. II.

Fig. I.

D

E

E

Column

A

B

Fig II

Fig IV

Fig III

Fig V.

Caution by the commanding officer.

Take Care to difplay Column to the Left !
The officers commanding platoons go to the
left, in order to conduct them.

To the Left,—Face !
The whole face to the left, except the front
platoon.

March !
The platoons faced, ftep off, and march ob.
liquely to their places in the line ; when the
fecond platoon has gained its proper diftance,
its officer commands

Halt ! Front ! To the Right,—Drefs !
dreffes his platoon with that already formed,
and takes his poft on the right : the other platoons form in the fame manner.

ARTICLE 3.

*The clofe Column formed on the Ground by the
Left, the Left in Front.*
[Plate II. Figure 3.]

This is formed in the fame manner as the
preceding column, only facing and marching to
the left inftead of the right. The officers will

D 3   conduct

conduct their platoons, and having dreſſed them, return to their poſts on the right.

A R T I C L E 4.

Diſplay of a Column formed by the Left, the Left in Front.

[Plate II. Figure 3.]

This column is uſually diſplayed to the right, on the ſame principles as the column formed to the right is diſplayed to the left.

A R T I C L E 5.

The cloſe Column formed on the Centre, or fifth Platoon, the Right in Front.

[Plate II. Figure 4.]

Caution.

Take Care to form Column on the fifth Platoon, the Right in Front !

To the Right and Left,—Face.

The fifth platoon ſtands faſt ; the others face to the centre ; the officers poſt themſelves at the head of their platoons, and break off ; and on receiving the word,

March !

conduct them to their poſts in the column ; the

four

four platoons on the right forming in the front, and the three platoons on the left forming in the rear of the fifth platoon.

When this column is to be formed with the left in front, the four platoons on the right form in the rear, and the three on the left form in front.

In all formations and difplayings, the officers whofe platoons march by the left, fo foon as they have dreffed their platoons in line or column, return to their pofts on the right.

A R T I C L E 6.

Difplay of a Column having the Right in Front, from the Centre, or fifth Platoon.
[Plate II. Figure 5.]

Caution.

Take Care to difplay Column from the Centre !

At this caution the officer of the platoon in front pofts a ferjeant on each flank of it, who are to remain there till the platoon on which the column difplays, has taken its poft in the line, when they retire along the rear of the battalion to their platoon.

To

To the Right and Left,—Face !

The four front platoons face to the right, the
fifth ſtands faſt, and the ſixth, ſeventh and
eighth face to the left.

March !

The four platoons of the right march to the
right, the firſt platoon taking care to march
ſtraight towards the point of view ; ſo ſoon as
the fourth platoon has unmaſked the fifth, its
officer commands,

Halt ! Front ! March !

and it marches up to its poſt in the line ; the
third and ſecond platoon, as ſoon as they have
reſpectively gained their diſtances, proceed in
the ſame manner ; and then the firſt halts and
dreſſes with them ; the fifth platoon in the
mean time marches to its poſt between the two
ſerjeants ; and the three platoons of the left
form by marching obliquely to their poſts in the
line, as before explained.

A R T I C L E 7.

*The cloſe Column formed by the Right, the Right
in Front, diſplayed to the Right.*

[Plate III. Figure 1.]

When

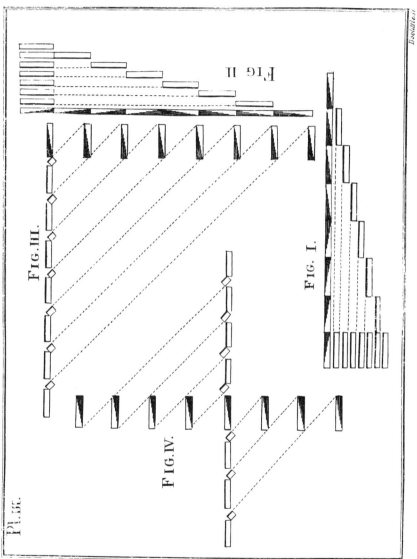

Fig. II

FIG.III.

FIG. I.

FIG.IV.

Pl. II.

When a column is formed by the right, and the nature of the ground will not permit its being difplayed to the left, it may be difplayed to the right in the following manner :

Caution.

Take Care to difplay Column to the Right !

The two ferjeants are to be pofted, as before, on the flanks of the front platoon.

To the Right,—Face !

The eighth platoon ftands faft, the reft face to the right, and march, the firft platoon keeping the line ; fo foon as the eighth platoon is unmafked, it marches forward to its poft between the two ferjeants of the firft platoon, left there for that purpofe ; the feventh platoon, having gained its diftance, halts, fronts and marches up to its ground ; the other platoons proceed in the fame manner, as explained in the difplay from the centre.

A R T I C L E 8.
The clofe Column formed by the Left, the Left in Front, difplayed to the Left.

[See Plate III. Figure 2.]

This is performed on the fame principles as the difplay of the column in the feventh article.

A

A column formed either by the right, left or centre, may, according to the ground, or any other circumſtance, be diſplayed on any particular platoon, on the principles before explained.

ARTICLE 9.

Open Columns

Are formed by wheeling to the right or left by platoons ; and, *when indiſpenſably neceſſary*, by marching the platoons by files, in the following manner :

Caution.

Take care to form open Columns by the Right !
[Plate III. Figure 3.]

To the Right,——Face !

The right platoon ſtands faſt, the reſt face to the right, and break off to the rear.

March !

Each platoon marches to its place in the column, the officers taking care to preſerve the proper diſtances between their platoons.

Open columns may in the ſame manner be formed by the left, centre, or on any particu-

lar

lar platoon, the officers taking care to preserve their proper diftances.

[See Plate 3. Figure 4]

Open columns are formed again in line, either by wheeling by platoons, or by clofing column and difplaying, as explained in the articles on clofe columns.

If the commanding officer chufes to clofe the open column, he will command

Clofe—Column! March!

On which the platoons march by the quick ftep, and clofe to within two paces of each other ; when the commanding officer of platoons fucceflively command

Halt! Drefs to the Right!

and the column is clofed.

When the commanding officers chufes to open a clofe column, he commands

Open—Column!

On which the front platoon advances, followed by the others fucceflively, as faft as they have their diftances.

The different manners of forming and difplaying columns being the bafis of all manœuvres,

nœuvres, require the greateft attention of both officers and men in the execution. The officers muft by frequent practice learn to judge of diftances with the greateft exactnefs ; as an augmentation or diminution of the proper diftance between the platoons, is attended with much confufion in forming a line. They muft alfo be very careful not to advance beyond the line, in forming battalion, but drefs their platoons carefully with the points of view.

ARTICLE 10.

Of Changing the Front of a Line,

The changing the front of a platoon, divifion, or even a battalion, may be performed by a fimple wheeling ; that of a brigade muft be performed by firft forming the open column, then marching it into the direction required, and forming the line.

If it be neceffary to change the front of a line confifting of more than a brigade, the fimpleft and fureft method is to form clofe columns, either by brigades or battalions, march them to the direction required, and difplay.

CHAPTER.

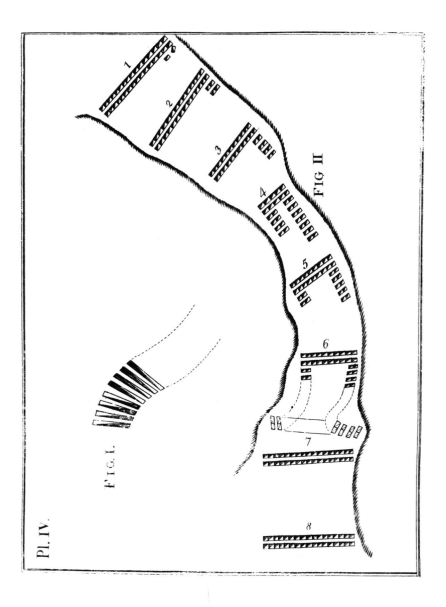

Pl. IV.

FIG. I.

FIG II

1

2

3

4

5

6

7

8

CHAPTER X.

Of the March of Columns.

THE march of columns is an operation fo
often repeated, and of fo much confe-
quence, that it muft be confidered as an effential article in the inftruction of both officers
and men.

ARTICLE 1.

The March of an open Column.
Column ! March !

The whole column muft always begin to
march, and halt, at the fame time, and only by
order of the commanding officer. After the firft
twenty paces he fhould command

Support—Arms !

When the men may march more at their
eafe, but keeping their files clofe. Before the
column halts, he fhould command

Carry—Arms ! Column ! Halt !
Drefs to the Right !

When marching in open column, the officer
commanding will often form battalion, by
wheeling to the right or left, in order to fee if
the officers have preferved the proper diftances
between the platoons.

E

A R T I C L E 2.

Columns changing the Direction of their March.

When a clofe column is obliged to change the direction of its march, the front platoon muft not wheel round on its flank, but advance in a direction more or lefs circular, according to the depth of the column, that the other platoons may follow.

[See Plate IV. Figure 1.]

An open column changes the direction of its march by wheeling the front platoon, the others following ; in doing which, the officers commanding platoons muft be particularly careful that their platoons wheel on the fame ground with the front platoon ; for which purpofe a ferjeant fhould be left to mark the pivot on which they are to wheel.

A R T I C L E 3.

Paffage of a Defile by a Column.

A column on its march coming to a defile, which obliges it to diminifh its front, the officer commanding the firft platoon commands

Break off!

On which thofe files which cannot pafs,break off,

off, face inwards, and follow their platoon by files, and as the defile narrows or widens more files will break off, or join the platoon : The fucceedng platoons proceed in the fame manner.

If the defile is difficult or long, fo foon as the front have paffed and gained fufficient ground, they will halt till the whole have paffed and formed, when they will continue the march.

ARTICLE 4.

A Column croffing a Plain, liable to be attacked by Cavalry.

When the commanding officer thinks himfelf in danger of being attacked by cavalry, he muft clofe the column, and on their approach, halt and face outwards ; the front platoon ftanding faft, the rear platoon going to the right about, and the others facing outwards from their centres.

In cafe of attack, the two firft ranks keep up a fmart running fire, beginning as well as ending by a fignal from the drum.

The foldiers muft be told, that under thefe circumftances, their fafety depends wholly on their courage ; the cavalry being only to be

E 2   dreaded

dreaded when the infantry ceafe to refift them.

When the column is to continue its march, the officer commands

Column ! To the Front,——Face ! March !
The platoons face to the front, and march.

A R T I C L E 5.

A Column marching by its Flank.

Column ! To the $\left\{\begin{array}{l}\textit{Right,}\\\textit{Left,}\end{array}\right\}$ *Face !*

If the column marches by the left, the officers go to the left of their refpective platoons.

March !
The column marches, dreffing by the right.

Column ! Halt ! Front !
The column faces to the front.

C H A P T E R XI.
Of the March in Line.

A R T I C L E I.
The March to the Front.
Battalion ! Forward !

AT this caution the enfign with the colours advances fix paces ; the ferjeant who
covered

covered him taking his place. The whole are to drefs by the colours. The commandant of the battalion will be pofted two paces in front of the colours, and will give the enfign an ob- ject to ferve as a direction for him to march ftraight forward.

March !

The enfign who carries the colours will be careful to march ftraight to the object given him by the colonel ; to do which, he muft fix on fome intermediate object.

If many battalions are in the line, the enfigns muft drefs by the enfign in the centre ; if only two, they will drefs by each other. They muft be very careful not to advance beyond the battalion they are to drefs by, it being much eafier to advance than to fall back.

Should a battalion by any caufe be hindered from advancing in line with the reft, the enfign of that battalion muft drop his colours, as a fignal to the other battalions (who might other- wife ftop to drefs by them) not to conform to their movements ; the colours to be raifed again when the battalion has advanced to its poft in the line.

E 3   The

The commanding officer of each battalion muſt be careful that his men dreſs and keep their files cloſe, and to preſerve the proper diſtances between his own battalion and thoſe on his flanks ; and when he finds that he is too near the one or the other, muſt command

Obliquely,—To the $\left\{\begin{matrix}\text{\textit{Right} !}\\ \text{\textit{Left} !}\end{matrix}\right.$

When the battalion will march by the oblique ſtep, as ordered, till they have recovered their diſtance, and receive the command

Forward !

Upon which the battalion will march forward, and the enſign take a new object to march to.

If the diſtance is augmented or diminiſhed only two, or three paces, the commanding officer will order the colours to incline a little, and then march forward ; the battalion conforming to their movement.

The officers commanding platoons will continually have an eye over them, immediately remedying any defect, carefully dreſſing with the centre, and keeping ſtep with the colours.

The officers in the rear muſt take care of the
ſecond

ſecond rank, remedying any defect in a low voice, and with as little noiſe as poſſible.

The ſoldier muſt not advance out of the rank the ſhoulder oppoſite the ſide he dreſſes to ; he muſt not crowd his right or left hand man, but give way to the preſſure of the cen- tre, and reſiſt that of the wings ; he muſt have his eyes continually fixed on the colours, turn- ing his head more or leſs, in proportion to his diſtance from them.

Battalion ! Halt !
The whole ſtop ſhort on the feet then ad- vanced.

Dreſs to the Right !
The men dreſs to the right, and the colours fall back into the ranks.

A R T I C L E 2.
Of the Charge with Bayonets.
The line marching, the commanding officer, on approaching the enemy, commands

March ! March !
On which the whole advance by the quick ſtep.

Charge—

Charge——Bayonet !

The line charge their bayonets, and quicken their ſtep ; the drums beat the long roll ; and the officers and men muſt take care to dreſs to the centre, and not crowd or open their files.

Battalion ! Slow Step !

The battalion fall into the ſlow ſtep, and carry their arms.

Halt ! Dreſs to the Right !

The battalion halts and dreſſes to the right.

A R T I C L E 3.

Method of paſſing any Obſtacle in Front of a Line.

When an obſtacle preſents itſelf before any diviſion, platoon, or number of files, the officer commanding the platoons, &c. commands

Break off !

on which the files obſtructed face outwards from their centre, and follow by files the platoons on their right and left ; if the platoons on the wings are obſtructed, they will face inwards, and follow in the ſame manner.

In proportion as the ground permits, the files will march up to their places in front, dreſs, and take ſtep with the colours.

ARTICLE

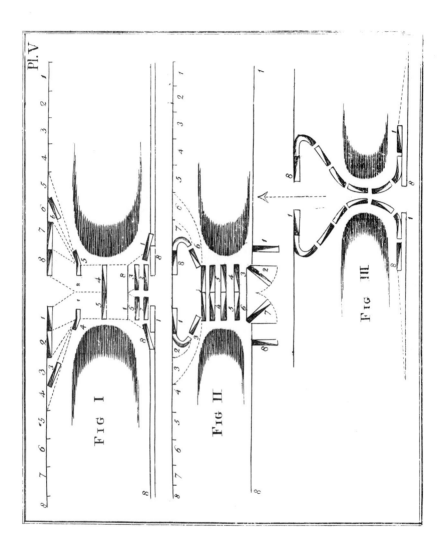

Pl. V

Fɪɢ I

Fɪɢ II

Fɪɢ III

ARTICLE 4.

Paffage of a Defile in Front, by Platoons.

A battalion marching and meeting with a bridge or defile, over or through which not more than the front of a divifion can pafs at a time, the commanding officer orders

Halt !

and then to the two platoons before whom the defile prefents itfelf

March !

on which they pafs the defile in one divifion. As foon as thofe two platoons have marched, the commanding officer orders

To the Right and Left,—Face !

The platoons on the right face to the left, and thofe on the left face to the right.

March !

They march till they join, fronting the defile ; when the commanding officer of the two platoons commands

Halt ! Front ! March !

and they pafs the defile ; the reft following in the fame manner.

As

As soon as the front divifion has paffed, it will halt ; and the other divifions, as faft as they arrive in the rear, face outwards, and march by files till they come to their proper places in battalion ; when the officers commanding the platoons order

Halt ! Front ! Drefs !

and the platoons drefs in line with thofe already formed.

ARTICLE 5.
Paffage of a Defile in Front, by Files.

If the defile will not permit more than four files to pafs, the four files before which the defile prefents itfelf enter without any word of command ; the reft face inwards, and follow them ; the whole marching through by files.

As foon as the files which firft entered, have paffed, they halt ; the others, as faft as they pafs, marching to their places in battalion.

ARTICLE 6.

Of the March in Retreat.
Battalion ! To the Right about,—Face !

The whole face to the right about ; the officers keeping their pofts.

Forward,—

Forward,—March !

The colours advance fix paces, and the whole ftep off, dreffing by them.

The paffage of any obftacle in retreat, is the fame as in the march to the front.

ARTICLE 7.

Paffage of a Defile in Retreat, by Platoons.

If it is at any time neceffary to pafs a defile in the rear, in prefence of an enemy, the line muft march as near as poffible to the defile; when the commanding officer orders

To the Front,—Face !
From the Wings,—By Platoons,—Pafs the Defile in the Rear !

The two platoons on the wings face outwards.

March !

The two platoons wheel by files, and march along the rear of the battalion to the entrance of the defile ; where joining, their officers command

Halt ! To the $\begin{Bmatrix} Right, \\ Left, \end{Bmatrix}$ *Face !*

The platoon of the right wing faces to the left ; the other platoon faces to the right ; and

both

both pafs in one divifion ; the other platoons following in the fame manner, except thofe of the centre.

When all have entered but the two centre platoons, that on the right faces to the right about, and marches twenty paces into the defile ; when the officer commands

Halt ! To the Right about,—Face !

The officer of the other platoon, when he fees them faced, will retire in the fame manner ; and having paffed twenty paces beyond the platoon halted in the defile, comes alfo to the right about ; they continuing in this manner to cover each other's retreat till they have paffed, when they face to the front, and cover the defile.

The three platoons of the right wing wheel to the left ; thofe of the left wing wheel to the right ; and having gained their proper diftances, the commanding officer orders

Halt !——Platoons !
To the Right and Left,—Wheel ! March !

The right wing wheels to the left, and the left to the right ; which forms the battalion.

If

If the defile fhould prefent itfelf behind any
other part of the battalion, the platoons fartheft
off muft always retreat firft ; and if the defile
becomes narrower than at the entrance, the platoons muft double behind each other.

A R T I C L E 8.

Paffage of a Defile in Retreat, by Files.

This manœuvre is performed in the fame
manner as the preceding, except that, inftead
of forming at the entrance, the platoons pafs
by files ; and having paffed, face to the right
and left, march till they have their proper diftances, and then wheel and form battalion.

The paffage of defiles may be executed at
firft in the common ftep, for the inftruction of
the troops ; in fervice, always in the quick
ftep.

The paffage of defiles being difficult in prefence of an enemy, the officers muft be particularly careful to keep the files clofed ; to be
quick in giving the words of command ; and
not lofe any time in the execution.

This manœuvre fhould always be covered by
troops pofted on each fide the defile, and on

F   every

every advantageous piece of ground that prefents itfelf, to annoy and keep back the enemy.

ARTICLE 9.

Method of paffing the front Line to the Rear.

The firſt line being obliged to retreat, will
face to the right about, and retire in line.

The fecond line, if not already formed in columns, will immediately, on perceiving the firſt
line retire, form in that order by brigades or
battalions ; and the firſt line having paffed the
intervals between the columns, the fecond line
will difplay ; or, if too clofely preffed by the
enemy, attack in columns the flanks of the battalions which purfue, thereby giving time for
the firſt line to form and take a new pofition.

CHAPTER XII.

*Of the Difpofition of the Field-pieces attached to
the Brigades.*

THE field-pieces attached to the different
brigades muſt always remain with them,
encamping on their right, unlefs the quarter-
maſter general thinks proper to place them on
any advantageous piece of ground in front.

When

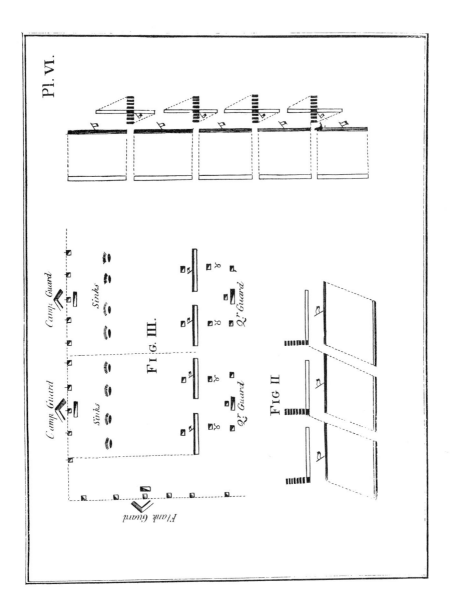

Pl. VI.

Camp Guard

Camp Guard

Sinks

Sinks

FIG. III.

Qr Guard

Qr Guard

Flank Guard

FIG II

When the army marches by the right, the field-pieces muſt march at the head of their reſpective brigades; when it marches by the left, they follow in the rear, unleſs circumſtances determine the general to order otherwiſe; but, whether they march in front, centre or rear of their brigades, they muſt always march between the battalions, and never between the platoons.

In manœuvring they muſt alſo follow their brigades, performing the manœuvres and evolutions with them; obſerving that, when the cloſe column is formed, they muſt always proceed to the flank of the column oppoſed to that ſide their brigade is to diſplay to; and on the column's diſplaying, they follow the firſt diviſion of their brigade; and when that halts and forms, the field-pieces immediately take their poſts on its right.

CHAPTER XIII.
Of the Firings.

WHEN the troops are to exerciſe with powder, the officers muſt carefully inſpect the arms and cartridge boxes, and take away all the cartridges with ball.

The

The firft part of the general will be the fignal for all firing to ceafe ; on the beating of which the officers and non-commiffioned officers muft fee that their platoons ceafe firing, load and fhoulder as quick as poffible. The commanding officer will continue the fignal till he fees that the men have loaded and fhouldered.

ARTICLE 1.

Firing by Battalion.
Caution.
Take Care to fire by Battalion !
Battalion ! Make ready ! Take Aim ! Fire !

If there be more than one battalion to fire, they are to do it in fucceffion from right to left ; but after the firft round, the odd battalions fire fo foon as the refpective battalions on their left begin to fhoulder ; and the even battalions fire when the refpective battalions on their right begin to fhoulder.

ARTICLE 2.

Firing by Divifions and Platoons.
Caution.
Take Care to fire by Divifions !
Divifion ! Make ready ! Take Aim ! Fire !

They fire in the fame order as is prefcribed for battalions in Article 1.

The

The firing by platoons is alfo executed in the fame order in the wings of the battalion, beginning with the right of each : that is, the firft and fifth platoons give the firft fire, the fecond and fixth the fecond fire, the third and feventh the third fire, and the fourth and eighth the fourth fire ; after which they fire as before prefcribed.

ARTICLE 3

Firing Advancing.

The battalion advancing receives the word,
Battalion ! Halt !
Take Care to fire by Divifions !
They fire as before.

ARTICLE 4.

Firing Retreating.

When a battalion is obliged to retire, it muft march as long as poffible ; but if preffed by the enemy, and obliged to make ufe of its fire, the commanding officer will order,

Battalion ! Halt !
To the Right about,—Face !
and fire by battalion, divifion, or platoon, as before directed.

F 3　　　　　　　CHAPTER

C H A P T E R   XIV.

Of the March of an Army or Corps.

THE greateſt attention on the part of the officers is neceſſary at all times, but more particularly on a march : The ſoldiers being then permitted to march at their eaſe, with the ranks and files open, without the greateſt care, theſe get confounded one with another ; and if ſuddenly attacked, inſtead of being able to form immediately in order of battle, the whole line is thrown into the utmoſt confuſion.

The order for the march of an army being given, the adjutant general will appoint the field officers for the advanced and rear guards, and iſſue orders to the brigade majors to have ready their reſpective quotas of other officers and men for the advanced guard, which will conſiſt of the number neceſſary for the guards of the new camp. Theſe, together with a pioneer of each company, and a ſerjeant from the regiment to conduct them, muſt be warned the evening before.

At the beating of the general, the troops are immediately to ſtrike their tents, and load the waggons, which muſt then fall into the line of march for the baggage.   At

At this fignal alſo all general and ſtaff officers guards, and thoſe of the commiſſaries, muſt return to their reſpective regiments.

At the beating of the aſſembly, the troops will aſſemble, and be formed in battalion on their reſpective parades.

The guards ordered, muſt then be conducted by the brigade majors, or adjutants of the day, to the rendezvous appointed for the advanced guard, where the field officers warned for that duty, will form them in battalions, or other corps, according to their ſtrength, and divide them regularly into diviſions and platoons. The officer commanding the advanced guard, muſt take care to have a guide with him, and to get every neceſſary information of the road.

The camp guards muſt at the ſame time retire to the rendezvous appointed for the rear guard, where they muſt be formed in the ſame manner.

At the ſame time alſo the quarter-maſters and pioneers of each battalion muſt aſſemble on the ground appointed for the advanced guard, where one of the deputies of the quarter-maſter
general

general muft form them in platoons, in the fame order as their refpective battalions march in the column.

Each detachment will be conducted by its quarter-mafter, who muft be anfwerable that it marches in the order prefcribed ; and the quarter-mafters of brigades will conduct thofe of their refpective brigades, and be anfwerable for their behaviour.

The fignal for marching being given, the whole will wheel by platoons or fections, as fhall be ordered, and begin the march.

The advanced guard will march at a diftance from the main body proportioned to its ftrength, having a patrole advanced ; and muft never enter any defile, wood, &c. without having firft examined it, to avoid falling into an ambufcade.

The pioneers are to march behind the advanced guard, and muft repair the roads, that the column may be obliged to file off as little as poffible.

The advanced guard, befides its patroles in front, muft have a flank guard, compofed of a

file

file from each platoon, and commanded by an officer, or non-commiſſioned officer, to march at the diſtance of one hundred paces on the flank, and keep up with the head of the advanced guard.

If it be neceſſary to have a flank guard on each ſide, a file muſt be ſent from the other flank of each platoon to compoſe it ; and as this ſervice is fatiguing, the men ſhould be relieved every hour. The like flank guards are to be detached from each battalion, in the column.

For the greater convenience of the ſoldiers, the ranks muſt be opened to half diſtance during the march.

When the column meets with a defile, or any obſtacle, the commanding officer muſt ſtop till the column has paſſed it, taking care that they paſs in as great order and as quick as poſſible ; and when one half have marched through, he muſt command the front to halt, till the whole have paſſed and formed, when he will continue the march.

When a column croſſes a road that leads to

the

the enemy, the patroles or guards on the flanks of the firft battalion muft form on the road, and halt till the patroles of the next battalion come up, which muft do the fame : The others pro- ceed in the fame manner, till the whole have paffed.

When the commanding officer thinks proper to halt on the march, immediately on the co- lumn's halting, the advanced, flank and rear guards muft form a chain of fentinels, to pre- vent the foldiers from ftraggling ; and all ne- ceffaries, as wood, water, &c. muft be fetched by detachments, as in camp.

On the beating the long roll, the whole are to form and continue the march.

On the march no orders are to be communi- cated by calling out, but muft be fent by the adjutants from regiment to regiment. The fig- nals for halting, marching flower and quicker, muft be given by beat of drum. (*See Chap.* xxi.)

The commanding officer of the advanced guard being informed by the quarter-mafter general, or his deputy, of the ground the troops are to encamp on, will go a head and reconnoitre it ; and immediately on the arrival of the advanced

guard,

guard, poſt his guards and ſentinels, as directed
in Chapter XXII.

March by Sections of Four.

The roads being very often two narrow to
admit the front of a platoon, and the troops being therefore continually obliged to break off,
which fatigues the men ; to prevent this, when
the road is not ſufficiently large throughout,
the battalions may be divided into ſections in
the following manner :

Each platoon is to be told off into ſections of
four files ; if there remain three files, they
form a ſection ; if two files, or leſs, they form
one rank. At the word,

By Sections of Four !
To the Right,—Wheel ! March !

they wheel by fours and march, the ſecond
rank of each ſection taking two paces diſtance
from the front rank. The officers commanding
platoons take poſt on the left of their firſt ſection ; but on the right, if the ſections wheel
to the left. The file-cloſers fall in on the flanks.

The officers muſt take great care that the
diſtance of two paces, and no more, is kept be.
tween the ranks. At the word,

Halt !

Halt !

The front rank of each fection ftops fhort and the fecond rank clofes up, which gives the proper diftance between the fections ; and by wheeling to the right or left the line is formed : or, if the commanding officer choofes, he may form platoons by the oblique ftep.

If a column be already on the march by platoons, and the road becomes too narrow and inconvenient to continue in that order, it may be formed into fections of four, in the following manner :

Caution by the commanding officer.

Take Care to break off by Sections of Four !
Upon which the officers commanding platoons tell them off as before, but without halting.

At the word
Sections of Four ! Break off !
the fections on the right of each platoon incline by the oblique ftep to the left ; and thofe on the left of each platoon, following the former, incline to the right, till they all cover ; when they march forward, opening the ranks as before directed. If the number of fections in a platoon be uneven, that in the centre is to
march

march ſtraight forward; the ſections on the right inclining to the left, and covering it in front; and thoſe on the left inclining to the right, and covering it in the rear.

CHAPTER XV.

Of the Baggage on a March.

THE inconveniencies ariſing to an army from having too great a number of waggons, muſt be evident to every officer; and it is expected, that for the future each officer will curtail his baggage as much as poſſible.

The order of march for the army will always determine that for the baggage; and, whatever place it may occupy in the line of march, the waggons muſt always follow in the ſame order as their reſpective regiments.

The quarter-maſter general, or his deputy, will give the order of march for the baggage, and the commander in chief will order an eſcort, to be commanded by a field officer, according to its ſtrength.

An officer of each battalion muſt be appointed to ſuperintend the ſtriking of the tents, and

G

loading

loading the waggons : he muſt ſee that the tents are properly tied up ; that no proviſions or other articles are packed in them ; and that the tent-poles are tied in a bundle by themſelves : he muſt not ſuffer the waggons to be overloaded, or any thing put into them but what is allow-ed ; and when the waggons are loaded, he muſt ſend them with the quarter-maſter ſerjeant to the rendezvous of the brigade. This ſerjeant is to remain with the baggage of his regiment, to ſee that the waggons follow in order ; and if a waggon breaks down, it muſt be put out of the line, that it may not impede the march of the reſt.

Each regiment will furniſh a non-commiſſion-ed officer to conduct the ſick and lame who are not able to march with their regiments. Theſe men are to repair, at the beating of the general, to the rendezvous appointed, where a ſufficient number of empty waggons will be ordered to attend for the reception of their knapſacks, and their arms, if neceſſary. A ſurgeon of each brigade is to attend the ſick belonging to it.

The commanding officer of each battalion will inſpect the ſick before they are ſent from the battalion, in order that none may be ſent but
thoſe

thofe who are really incapable of marching with their regiments. And the officer commanding the efcort will be anfwerable that no foldiers are permitted to march with the baggage on any pretence whatever, except the quarter-mafter ferjeant of each regiment, as before directed.

No waggons are to be permitted to go between the battalions or brigades, except the ammunition waggons.

The waggons of the park, and others, are to be conducted agreeably to the foregcing directions, and the neceffary officers furnifhed to keep order on the march.

CHAPTER XVI.
The Manner of laying out a Camp, with the Order of Encampment.

WHEN the quarter-mafters arrive on the ground where the troops are to encamp, the quarter-mafter general having fixed his line of encampment, will conduct them along the line, and give each brigade quarter-mafter the ground neceffary for his brigade.

The quarter-mafters of regiments will then have their ground given them by the brigade

G 2   quarter

quarter-mafters, and will mark out the place for each company and tent, and for the kitchens, &c. &c. as defcribed in the following order :

Order of Encampment.
[Plate VII and VIII.]

The infantry will on all occafions encamp by battalions, as they are formed in order of battle.

The front of the camp will occupy the fame extent of ground as the troops when formed ; and the intervals between the battalions will be twenty paces, with an addition of eight paces for every piece of cannon a battalion may have.

The quarter-mafter of each regiment fhall be anfwerable that he demands no more ground than is neceffary for the number of men he has actually with the regiment, allowing two feet for each file, exclufive of the officers, and adding fixteen feet for the intervals between the platoons. He is alfo to be anfwerable that no more tents are pitched than are abfolutely neceffary, allowing one tent for the non-commiffioned officers of each company; and one for every fix men, including the drums and fifes.

The tents of the non-commiffioned officers and privates are to be pitched in two ranks,
with

with an interval of six paces between the ranks, and two feet between each tent : the tents of the non-commiffioned officers to be in the front rank, on the right of their companies, in the right wing, and on the left in the left wing of the battalion. Nine feet front are to be allowed for each tent with its interval, and twenty feet in the centre of the battalion for the adjutant ; but when a regiment forms two battalions, the adjutant is to encamp with the firft battalion, the ferjeant major fupplying his place in the fecond.

The captains and fubalterns tents are to be in one line, twenty feet from the rear of the mens tents ; the captains in the right wing oppofite the right of their refpective companies, and the fubalterns oppofite the left ; and the contrary in the the left wing.

The field officers tents are to be in one line, thirty feet from the line of officers ; the colonel's oppofite the centre ; the lieutenant colonel's on the right ; and the major's on the left. But if the regiment forms two battalions, the colonel encamps behind the centre of the firft battalion ; the lieutenant-colonel behind the fecond battalion ; and the major behind the interval between the two battalions.

The

The furgeon, pay-mafter, and quarter-mafter, encamp in one line, with the front of their tents in a line with the rear of the field officers tents; the furgeon on the right, pay-mafter on the left, and quarter-mafter in the centre.

The kitchens are to be dug behind their refpective companies, forty feet from the field officers tents. The futlers tents are to be between the kitchens.

The horfes and waggons are to be placed in a line, twenty feet behind the kitchens.

The drums of each battalion are to be piled fix paces in front of the adjutant's tent, and the colours planted before them.

The camp guards are to be three hundred paces in front of the firft line, and the fame diftance in the rear of the fecond line.

The quarter guard is to be forty feet from the waggons, oppofite the interval between the two battalions who furnifh it.

The finks of the firft line are to be three hundred feet in front, and thofe of the fecond line the fame diftance in the rear of the camp.

The commanding officers of regiments are to
be

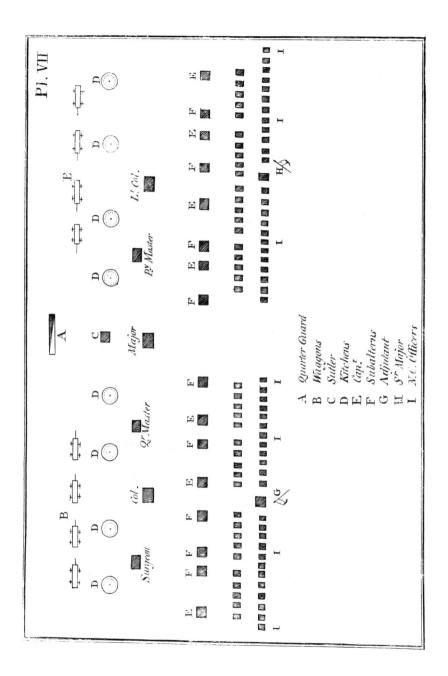

Pl. VII

A Quarter Guard
B Wagons
C Sutler
D Kitchens
E Cap.ᵗ
F Subalterns
G Adjutant
H S.ᵗ Major
I N.C. Officers

Surgeon

Col.

Q.ᵣ Master

Major

Pa.ᵣ Master

L.ᵗ Col.

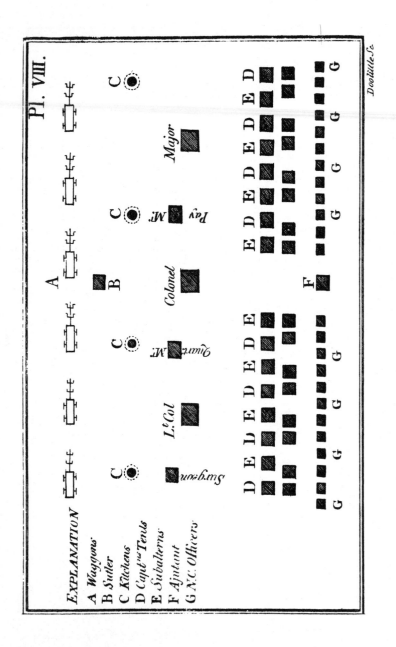

Pl. VIII.

EXPLANATION

A Waggons
B Sutler
C Kitchens
D Capt⁽ⁿˢ⁾ Tents
E Subalterns
F Ajutant
G N.C. Officers

Doolittle Sc.

be anfwerable that no tents are pitched out of the line of encampment on any account whatever, except for the regimental hofpital.

The ground being marked out, the quartermafters will leave the pioneers, and go to meet their regiments, conduct them to their ground, and inform the colonel where they are to go for their neceffaries.

CHAPTER XVII.
Manner of entering a Camp.

THE head of the column arriving at the entrance of the camp, the commanding officer of the firft battalion will command

Carry——Arms !

On which the men carry their arms, and the drums beat a march ; and the officers will fee that their platoons have their proper diftances, clofe the ranks and files, and each drefs the flank on which his platoon is to wheel, with the fame flank of the platoon preceding. The other battalions obferve the fame directions, and keep their proper diftances from each other.

The general or officer commanding muft take great care to march the troops in a direct line
along

along the front of the camp, and at such a diftance as to give sufficient room for the largeft
platoons to march clear of the line of tents.

As the battalions refpectively arrive in front
of their ground, they halt, form battalion,
(dreffing with the right) and order or fupport
their arms.

The adjutants immediately turn out the piquets that may have been ordered, form them
in front of their refpective battalions, and fend
them to the rendezvous appointed.

The piquets being fent off, the commanding
officers of battalions command their men to pile
their arms, and difmifs them to pitch their tents.

As foon as a company have pitched their
tents, the captain parades them, and they fetch
in their arms.

The tents of the battalion being all pitched, the
adjutant will form the detachments for neceffaries, and fend them off.

In the mean time the commanding officer of
the battalion, having examined the ground, will,
if necelfary, order out a party to open the communications on the right and left ; in front for
the troops, and in the rear for the baggage.

CHAPTER

CHAPTER XVIII.

Neceffary Regulations for preferving Order and Cleanlinefs in the Camp.

WHEN a regiment enters a camp, the field officers muft take care that the encampment is pitched regularly ; that the finks and kitchens are immediately dug in their proper places ; and that no tents are pitched in any part of the camp contrary to the order prefcribed.

At leaft one officer of a company muft remain on the parade to fee that the tents are pitched regularly on the ground marked out.

The tents fhould be marked with the name of each regiment and company, to prevent their being loft or exchanged, and the tents of each company numbered ; and each non-commiffioned officer fhould have a lift of the tents, with the mens names belonging to each.

The utenfils belonging to the tents are to be carried alternately by the men ; and the non-commiffioned officers of the fquads are to be anfwerable that they are not loft or fpoiled.

Whenever a regiment is to remain more than one night on the fame ground, the foldiers muft be obliged to cut a fmall trench round their

tents,

tents, to carry off the rain ; but great care muſt be taken they do not throw the dirt up againſt the tents.

One officer of a company muſt every day viſit the tents ; ſee that they are kept clean ; that every utenſil belonging to them is in proper order ; and that no bones or other filth be in or near them : and when the weather is fine, ſhould order them to be ſtruck about two hours at noon, and the ſtraw and bedding well aired.

The ſoldiers ſhould not be permitted to eat in their tents, except in bad weather ; and an officer of a company muſt often viſit the meſſes ; ſee that the proviſion is good and well cooked ; that the men of one tent meſs together ; and that the proviſion is not ſold or diſpoſed of for liquor.

A ſubaltern, four non-commiſſioned officers and a drummer muſt every day be appointed for the police of each battalion, who are on no account to be abſent during the time they are on duty.

The officer of the police is to make a general inſpection into the cleanlineſs of the camp, not ſuffer fire to be made any where but in the kitchens, and cauſe all dirt to be immediately re- removed,

moved, and either burnt or buried. He is to be prefent at all diftributions in the regiment, and to form and fend off all detachments for neceffaries.

In cafe the adjutant is obliged to be abfent, the officer of the police is to do his duty till his retun ; and for that purpofe he muft attend at the adjutant's tent, to be ready to receive and diftribute any orders that may come for the regiment.

The drummer of the police muft attend conftantly at the adjutant's tent, to be ready at all times to communicate the neceffary fignals; nor muft he abfent himfelf on any account during the twenty-four hours, without leaving another drummer to fupply his place till his return, nor then, without leave from the adjutant.

When any of the men want water, they muft apply to the officer of the police, who will order the drum to beat the neceffary fignal; on which all who want water muft immediately parade with their canteens before the colours, where the officer of the police will form and fend them off under the care of two non-commiffioned officers of the police, who are to be anfwerable that

they

they bring back the whole detachment, and that no exceffes are committed whilft they are out. Wood and all other neceffaries muft be fetched in the fame manner. Except in cafe of neceffity, not more than one detachment is to be out at a time.

The quarter-mafter muft be anfwerable that the parade and environs of the encampment of a regiment are kept clean ; that the finks are filled up, and new ones dug every four days, and oftner in warm weather ; and if any horfe or other animal dies near the regiment, he muft caufe it to be carried at leaft half a mile from camp, and buried.

The place where the cattle are killed muft be at leaft fifty paces in the rear of the waggons ; and the entrails and other filth immediately buried ; for which the commiffaries are to be anfwerable.

The quarter-mafter general muft take care that all dead animals, and every other nuifance in the environs of the camp, be removed.

No

No non-commiffioned officer or foldier fhall be permitted to pafs the chain of fentinels round the camp, without permiffion in writing from the commanding officer of his regiment or battalion ; which permiffion fhall be dated the fame day, and fhall, on the return of the perfon to whom it was granted, be delivered to the adjutant, who is to return it to the colonel or commanding officer, with his report.

Every detachment not conducted by a commiffioned officer, fhall have a written permiffion from a field officer, or officer commanding a regiment, or the officer of the police if it be a detachment going for neceffaries ; without which they are not to be permitted to pafs the chain.

All officers whatever are to make it a point of duty to ftop every non-commiffioned officer or foldier they meet without the chain, and examine his pafs ; and if he has not a fufficient pafs, or having one is committing any excefs, the officer muft conduct him to the neareft guard, from whence he muft be fent, with his crime, to his regiment.

The fentinel before the colours muft have orders, in cafe he hears any alarm in camp, or

H   at at the advanced pofts, to acquaint the adjutant with it ; who will inform the commanding officer of the battalion, or order an alarm beat, if the cafe requires it.

CHAPTER XIX.
Of Roll-Calls.

THE rolls fhall be called in each battalion at troop and retreat beating, at which times the men are to parade with their arms ; and at the beating of the *reveille*, and at noon, the commanding officers of companies fhall caufe the rolls of their refpective companies to be called, the men parading for that purpofe without arms, and to be detained no longer than is neceffary to call the roll.

The non-commiffioned officers are to vifit their refpective fquads a quarter of an hour after *tattoo* beating ; fee that they are all prefent and retired to reft ; and make their report to the commanding officer of the company.

No non-commiffioned officer or foldier is to be abfent from roll-call without permiffion from the commanding officer of the company.

No commiffioned officer is to be abfent from roll-call without permiffion from the commanding officer of the regiment.   CHAPTER

CHAPTER XX.

Of the Inspection of the Men, their Dress, Neceffaries, Arms, Accoutrements and Ammunition.

THE oftener the foldiers are under the infpection of their officers the better ; for which reafon every morning at troop beating they muft infpect into the drefs of their men ; fee that their clothes are whole and put on properly ; their hands and faces wafhed clean ; their hair combed ; their accoutrements properly fixed, and every article about them in the greateft order. Thofe who are guilty of repeated neglects in thefe particulars are to be confined and punifhed.—The field officers muft pay attention to this object, taking proper notice of thofe companies where a vifible neglect appears, and publicly applauding thofe who are remarkable for their good appearance.

Every day the commanding officers of companies muft examine their men's arms and ammunition, and fee that they are clean and in good order. [*See farther Chap.* XXIII.]

That the men may always appear clean on the parade, and as a means of preferving their

H 2   health,

health, the non-commiffioned officers are to fee that they wafh their hands and faces every day, and oftener when neceffary. And when any river is nigh, and the feafon favourable, the men fhall bathe themfelves as frequently as poffible, the commanding officers of each battalion fending them by fmall detachments fucceffively, under the care of a non-commiffioned officer; but on no account muft the men be permitted to bathe when juft come off a march, at leaft till they have repofed long enough to get cool.

Every Saturday morning the captains are to make a general infpection of their companies, and examine into the ftate of the men's neceffaries, obferving that they agree in quantity with what is fpecified in the company book; and that every article is the man's who fhews it: For which purpofe, and to difcover theft, every man's things fhould be marked; if any thing is deficient, ftrict enquiry muft be made into the caufe of it; and fhould it appear to be loft, pledged, fold or exchanged, the offender muft be feverely punifhed.

That the men may not be improperly burdened and fatigued, the captains are not to fuffer them to carry any thing which is either ufelefs or unneceffary.   CHAPTER

CHAPTER XXI.

Of the different Beats of the Drum.

THE different daily beats ſhall begin on the right, and be inſtantly followed by the whole army ; to facilitate which, the drummer's call ſhall be beat by the drums of the police, a quarter of an hour before the time of beating, when the drummers will aſſemble before the colours of their reſpective battalions ; and as ſoon as the beat begins on the right, it is to be immediately taken up by the whole army, the drummers beating along the front of their reſpective battalions, from the centre to the right, from thence to the left, and back again to the centre, where they finiſh.

The different beats and ſignals are to be as follows :

The General is to be beat only when the whole are to march, and is the ſignal to ſtrike the tents, and prepare for the march.

The Aſſembly is the ſignal to repair to the colours.

The March for the whole to move.

The Reveille is beat at day-break, and is the ſignal for the ſoldiers to riſe, and the centries to leave off challenging.

H 3

The Troop affembles the foldiers together, for the purpofe of calling the roll and infpecting the men for duty.

The Retreat is beat at fun-fet, for calling the roll, warning the men for duty, and reading the orders of the day.

The Tattoo is for the foldiers to repair to their tents, where they muft remain till *reveille* beating next morning.

To Arms is the fignal for getting under arms in cafe of alarm.

The Parley is to defire a conference with the enemy.

The Signals.

Adjutant's call—*firft part of the troop.*

Firft Serjeant's call—*one roll and three flams.*

All non-commiffioned officers call—*two rolls and five flams*

To go for wood—*poing ftroke and ten-ftroke roll.*

water—*two ftrokes and a flam.*

provifions—*roaft beef.*

Front to halt—*two flams from right to left, and a full drag with the right, a left hand flam and a right hand full drag.*

For

For the front to advance quicker—*the long march.*

to march flower—*the taps.*

For the drummers—*the drummers call.*

For a fatigue party—*the pioneers march.*

For the church call—*the parley.*

The drummers will practife a hundred paces in front of the battalion, at the hours fixed by the adjutant general ; and any drummer found beating at any other time, (except ordered) fhall be punifhed.

C H A P T E R XXII.
Of the Service of the Guards.
A R T I C L E I.
Of the different Guards, with their Ufe.

THE different guards of the army will confift of

1ft. Out poft and piquet guards.

2d. Camp and quarter guards.

3d. General and ftaff officers guards.

The piquet guards are formed by detachments from the line, and are pofted at the avenues of the camp, in fuch numbers as the general commanding thinks neceffary for the fecurity of the camp.

The

The camp and quarter guards are for the better fecurity of the camp, as well as for preferving good order and difcipline.

Every two battalions will furnifh a camp and quarter guard between them, to confift of

Subalt.	Serj.	Corp.	Drumm.	Priv.	
1.	1.	1.	1.	27.	{ For the camp guard.
-	-	1.	-	9.	{ For the quarter guard.

The camp guard of the front line is to be pofted three hundred paces in front of it, and that of the fecond line the fame diftance in the rear of the fecond line, each oppofite the interval of the two battalions who furnifh it.

Each guard will poft nine fentinels, viz. one before the guard, two on the right and two on the left ; thefe five fentinels, with thofe from the other battalions, forming a chain in front and rear of the camp ; the fixth and feventh fentinels before the colours ; and the eighth and ninth before the tents of the commanding officers of the two battalions.

In order to complete the chain of fentinels round the camp, the adjutant general will order two flank guards from the line, to confift of a commiffioned officer, and as many men as are neceffary to form a chain on the flanks.

The

The intention of the camp guards being to form a chain of fentinels round the camp, in order to prevent improper perfons entering, or the foldiers going out of camp, the commanding officers of brigades will add to, or diminifh them, fo as to anfwer the above purpofe.

The quarter guard is to be pofted twenty paces in the rear of the line of waggons, and will furnifh three fentinels ; viz. one at the guard, and one behind each battalion.

The guards of the general and other officers will be as follows :

	Sub.	Serj.	Corp.	Priv.
A major general will have	1	1	1	20
A brigadier general	0	1	1	12
Quarter-mafter general (as fuch)	0	1	1	12
Adjutant general -	0	1	1	12
Commiffary general -	0	0	1	6
Pay-mafter general -	0	0	1	6
Auditors - -	0	0	1	6
Judge advocate general -	0	0	1	3
Mufter-mafter general -	0	0	1	3
Clothier general -	0	0	1	3

Brigade commiffary ⎫
General hofpital ⎬ according to circumftances
Provoft guard ⎭

Any additional guard to the quarter-mafter,
commiffary

commiffary or clothier general, will be determined by the ftores they may have in poffeffion.

The different guards are all to mount at one hour, to be regulated by the commanding officer for the time being.

The camp and quarter guards are to parade before the interval of their battalions, where they will be formed by the adjutant who furnifhes the officer, and immediately fent off to their refpective pofts.

The guard of a major general is to be furnifhed from his own divifion, each brigade furnifhing it by turns ; it is to be formed by the major of brigade, and fent from the brigade parade.

The guard of a brigadier general is to be furnifhed by his own brigade, and formed and fent from the brigade parade by the major of brigade. The brigade commiffary's guard is to be furnifhed in the fame manner.

The other guards being compofed of detachments from the line by brigades, each detachment is formed on the brigade parade by the major of brigade, and fent with an adjutant to the grand parade.

All

All guards (except thofe which are honorary)
fhould ordinarily be of force proportioned to
the number of fentinels required, allowing
three relieves for each poft.

ARTICLE 2.
Of the Grand Parade.

As foon as a detachment arrives on the grand
parade, the officer having dreffed the ranks,
commands,

Order—Firelocks !

and then takes poft eight paces in front of his
detachment ; the non-commiffioned officers fall
two paces into the rear, except one who re-
mains on the right of every detachment. Each
detachment takes poft on the left of that preceding it, and is examined by the brigade major of the day as it arrives.

When the whole are affembled, the adjutant
of the day dreffes the line, counts the files from
right to left, and takes poft on the right.

The brigade major then commands,
Attention! Shoulder—Firelock ! Support—Arms !

Officers and Non-commiffioned Officers !
To the Centre—March !

The officers then march to the centre, and
form

form themfelves, according to feniority, in one rank, fixteen paces in front of the guards ; the non-commiffioned officers advance and form two ranks, four paces in the rear of the officers, and with the fame diftance between their ranks.

The brigade major then appoints the officers and non-commiffioned officers to their pofts ; the officers in the following manner :

The 1ft on the right of the	1ft
2d on the left of the	8th
3d in the centre, on the right of the	5th
4th on the right of the 2d divifion, or	3d
5th on the right of the 4th divifion, or	7th
6th on the right of the	2d
7th on the right of the	8th
8th on the right of the	4th
9th on the right of the	6th
10th in the rear of the	1ft
11th in the rear of the	8th
12th in the rear of the	5th
13th in the rear of the	3d
14th in the rear of the	7th
15th in the rear of the	2d
16th in the rear of the	6th
17th in the rear of the	4th
18th in the rear of the	5th
19th in the rear of the	1ft
20th in the rear of the	8th

The

The non-commiſſioned officers are poſted thus : A ſerjeant on the right of each platoon, and one on the left of the whole ; the reſt as file-cloſers equally divided to each platoon.

Whilſt this is doing, the adjutant divides the guard into eight platoons, leaving proper intervals between the platoons for the officers who are to command them.

The brigade major having appointed the officers, and the battalion being divided, he commands,

Officers and Non-commiſſioned Officers !
To your Poſts !

The officers and non-commiſſioned officers face outwards from the centre.

March !
They go directly to their poſts in the battalion.

The brigade major then advances to the general officer of the day, informs him that the battalion is formed, and takes his directions relative to the exerciſe.

The general of the day will uſually order the manual exerciſe to be performed, and ſome

I   manœuvres,

manœuvres, fuch as he thinks proper ; the major of brigade of the day giving the words of command.

The exercife being finifhed, the major of brigade commands,

Order—Firelocks!

The drums then beat from right to left of the parade, and paffing behind the officers of the day, take poft on their left.

The major of brigade then orders,

Shoulder—Firelocks ! Support—Arms !
Officers and Non-commiffioned Officers !
To the Centre—March !

They advance as before to the centre, and the brigade major appoints them to their refpective guards, takes the name of the officer commanding each guard, and gives him the parole and counterfign. The adjutant having in the mean time told off the guards, and divided them into platoons, the brigade major then commands,

Officers and Non-commiffioned Officers !
To your Pofts ! March !

The officers go to their refpective pofts.

The brigade major then commands,

Prefent—Arms !   And

And advancing to the general, acquaints him that the guards are formed ; and on receiving his orders to march them off, he commands,

Shoulder—Firelocks !
By Platoons ! To the Right—Wheel ! March !

The whole wheel, and march by the general, the officers faluting him as they pafs ; and when the whole have paffed, they wheel off and march to their refpective pofts.

A R T I C L E 3.

Of relieving Guards and Sentinels.

The guards in camp will be relieved every twenty-four hours. The guards without the limits of the camp will ordinarily be relieved in the fame manner ; but this muft depend on their diftances from camp, and other circumftances, which may fometimes require their continuing on duty for feveral days. In this cafe they muft be previoufly notified to provide themfelves accordingly.

The guards are to march in the greateft order to their refpective pofts, marching by platoons, whenever the roads will permit.

When the new guard approaches the poft,

I 2   they

they carry their arms ; and the officer of the old guard, having his guard paraded, on the approach of the new guard, commands,

Prefent—Arms !
and his guard prefent their arms.

The new guard marches paft the old guard, and takes poft three or four paces on its right (both guards fronting towards the enemy ;) and the officer command,

Prefent—Arms !
and the new guard prefent their arms.

The two officers then approach each other, and the relieving officer takes his orders from the relieved. Both officers then return to their guards, and commands,

Shoulder—Firelocks !
Non-commiffioned Officers ! Forward,—March !
The non-commiffioned officers of both guards, who are to relieve the fentinels, advance in front of the new guard.

The ferjeant of the new guard then tells off as many fentinels as are neceffary ; and the corporal of the new guard, conducted by a corporal of the old guard, relieves the fentinels, beginning by the guard-houfe. When

When the fentinel fees the relief approach, he prefents his arms, and the corporal halting his relief at fix paces diftance, commands,

Prefent—Arms!

Recover—Arms!

This laft command is only for the fentinel relieving, and the one to be relieved; the former immediately approaching with the corporal, and having received his orders from the old fentry, takes his place; and the fentry relieved marches into the ranks, placing himfelf on the left of the rear rank.

Front—Face!

Both fentries face to the front. The corporal then orders,

Shoulder—Firelocks! Support—Arms!

March!

and the relief proceeds in the fame manner till the whole are relieved.

If the fentries are numerous, the ferjeants are to be employed as well as the corporals in relieving them.

When the corporal returns with the old fentinels, he leads them before the old guard, and difmiffes them to their ranks.

I 3 The

The officer of the old guard then forms his guard in the fame manner as when he mounted, and marches them in order to camp.

As foon as he arrives in the camp, he halts, forms the men of the different brigades together, and fends them to their refpective brigades, conducted by a non-commiffioned officer, or careful foldier.

When the old guard march off, the new guard prefent their arms, till they are gone, then fhoulder, face to the left, and take the place of the old guard.

The officer then orders a non-commiffioned officer to take down the names of the guard, in the following manner :

Hours they go on,	10---4, 10---4.	12--6, 12--6.	2---8, 2---8.
	Men's names.	Men's names.	Men's names.
Poft No. 1.			
2.			
3.			
4.			
5.			
6.			
7.			
8.			

Suppofe the guard to confift of twenty-four men, and to furnifh eight fentinels, they are divided into three relieves, and the pofts being

numbered,

numbered (beginning always with the guard-houfe) each man's name is put down againft the number of the poft he will always ftand fentry at during the guard, by which means an officer knows what particular man was at any poft during any hour of the day or night.

The relief of fentries is always to be marched in the greateft order, and with fupported arms, the corporal often looking back to obferve the conduct of the men ; and if an officer approaches, he is to order his men to handle their arms, fupporting them again when he has paffed.

The corporals are to be anfwerable that the fentries, when relieving, perform their motions with the greateft fpirit and exactnefs.

A corporal who is detected in having the infolence to fuffer fentries to relieve each other, without his being prefent, fhall, as well as the fentry fo relieved, be feverely punifhed.

ARTICLE 4.

Inftructions to Officers on Guard.

On the vigilance of the officer depends not only the fafety of his guard, but that of the whole army.

As

As it is highly neceffary an officer fhould have
fome knowledge of his fituation, he muft, immediately after relieving the old guard, vifit
the fentinels, and examine the ground round
his poft ; and if he thinks the fentries not fufficient to fecure him from a furprife, he is at
liberty to place more, acquainting therewith
the general or field officer of the day who vi-
fits his poft ; but without their leave he is not
to alter any that are already pofted. He muft
caufe the roads leading to the enemy and to
the next pofts to be well reconnoitred by an
officer of the guard, or for want of one, by an
intelligent non-commiffioned officer and fome
faithful men, inform himfelf of every thing neceffary for his fecurity, and ufe every poffible
precaution againft a furprife. He muft permit
no ftranger to enter his poft, nor fuffer his
men to talk with him. If a fufpicious perfon,
or a deferter from the enemy approaches, he
muft ftop him and fend him to head quarters,
or to a fuperior officer. He muft on no account
fuffer the foldiers to pull off their accoutrements,
or ftraggle more than twenty paces from the
guard ; and if water or any other neceffaries
are wanted for the guard, they muft be fent for

by

by a non-commiffioned officer and fome men (with their arms if at an out-poft) on no account fuffering a foldier to go by himfelf ; but never whilft the fentinels are relieving. He muft examine every relief before it is fent off ; fee that their arms are loaded and in order, and that the men are acquainted with their duty ; and if by any accident a man fhould get the leaft difguifed with liquor, he muft on no account be fuffered to go on fentry.

At every relief the guard muft parade, and the roll be called ; and during the night (and when near the enemy, during the day) the guard muft remain under arms till the relief returns.

During the day the men may be permitted to reft themfelves as much as is confiftent with the fafety of the guard ; but in the night, no man muft be fuffered to lay down or fleep on any account, but have his arms conftantly in his hands, and be ready to fall in on the leaft alarm.

Between every relief the fentries muft be vifited by a non-commiffioned officer and a file of men ; and, when more than one officer is on guard, as often as poffible by an officer. A patrol alfo muft be frequently fent on the roads leading to the enemy. During

During the day, the fentinels on the out-pofts muſt ſtop every party of men, whether armed or not, till they have been examined by the officer of the guard.

As ſoon as it is dark, the counterſign muſt be given to the fentinels of the piquets and advanced pofts, after which they are to challenge all that approach them ; and if any perſon, after being ordered to ſtand, ſhould continue to approach or attempt to eſcape, the ſentry, after challenging him three times, muſt fire on him.

The fentinels of the interior guards of the camp will receive the counterſign, and begin to challenge, at ſuch hours as ſhall be determined in orders, according to circumſtances.

A fentinel, on perceiving any perſon approach, muſt challenge briſkly, and never ſuffer more than one to advance, till he has the counterſign given him ; if the perſon challenged has not the counterſign, the ſentry muſt call the ſerjeant of the guard, and keep the perſon at a little diſtance from his poſt, till the ſerjeant comes to examine him.

Whenever a ſentry on an out-poſt perceives more than three men approach, he muſt order
them

them to ftand, and immediately pafs the word
for the ferjeant of the guard ; the officer of the
guard muft immediately parade his guard, and
fend a ferjeant with a party of men to examine
the party : The non-commiffioned officer muft
order the commanding officer of the party to
advance, and conduct him to the officer of the
guard ; who, in cafe he is unacquainted with his
perfon, and does not choofe to truft either to
his cloathing or to his knowledge of the counterfign, muft demand his paffport, and examine
him ftrictly ; and if convinced of his belonging
to the army, muft let him pafs.

If a fentry, on challenging, is anfwered *relief*,
patrol or *round*, he muft in that cafe order the
ferjeant or corporal to advance with the counterfign ; and if he is then affured of their being
the relief, &c. he may fuffer them to advance.

A fentinel muft take the greateft care not to
be furprifed ; he muft never fuffer the perfon
who advances to give the counterfign, to approach within reach of his arms, and always
charge his bayonet.

The officers who mount the camp guards muft
give orders to their fentries not to fuffer any
perfon

perſon to paſs in or out of camp, except by one of the guards, nor then till the officer of the guard has examined him.

In caſe one of the guard deſerts, the officer muſt immediately change the counterſign, and ſend notice thereof to the general of the day ; who is to communicate the ſame to the other guards, and the adjutant general.

As ſoon as the officer of a guard diſcovers the approach of the enemy, he muſt immediately ſend notice to the neareſt general officer, call in the ſentries, and put himſelf in the beſt poſture of defence. If attacked on his poſt, he will defend it to the utmoſt of his power, nor retreat, unleſs compelled by ſuperior force ; and even then he muſt retire in the greateſt order, keeping a fire on the enemy, whoſe ſuperiority, however great, can never juſtify a guard's retiring in diſorder. Should the enemy purſue a guard into camp, the officer muſt take care to retire through the intervals of the battalions, and forming in the rear of the line, wait for further orders.

When an officer is poſted at a bridge, defile, or any work, with orders to maintain it, he muſt

defend

defend himself to the laft extremity, however fuperior the force of the enemy may be, as it is to be fuppofed that the general who gave thofe orders will reinforce him, or order him to retire whenever he thinks it proper.

An officer muft never throw in the whole of his fire at once ; for which reafon every guard is to be divided into two or more divifions or platoons, according to its ftrength ; any number above eight and under feventy-eight men forming two platoons ; the eldeft officer taking poft on the right of the firft platoon, the next eldeft on the right of the fecond platoon, and the third on the left of the whole ; the non-commiffioned officers cover the officers ; the drum is to be on the right of the captain, and the fentinel one pace advanced of the drum. If the guard confifts of no more than twelve men, it forms in one rank.

ARTICLE 5.

Method of going and receiving the Grand Rounds.

The general and field officers of the day will vifit the feveral guards during the day, as often and at fuch hours as they judge proper.

K   When

When the fentry before the guard perceives the officer of the day, he will call to the guard to turn out ; and the guard, being paraded, on the approach of the officer of the day prefent their arms.

The officer of the day will examine the guard ; fee that none are abfent ; that their arms and accoutrements are in order ; that the officers and non-commiffioned officers are acquainted with their duty ; and that the fentinels are properly pofted and have received proper orders.

Not only the officers of the day, but all general officers are at liberty to vifit the guards and make the fame examination.

The officers of the guard fhall give the parole to the officer of the day, if demanded.

During the night, the officers of the day will go the grand rounds.

When the officer of the day arrives at the guard from whence he intends to begin his rounds, he will make himfelf known as fuch by giving the officer of the guard the parole.—He will then order the guard under arms, and hav-

ing

ing examined it, demand an efcort of a ferjeant and two men, and proceed to the next poft.

When the rounds are challenged by a fenti-nel, they will anfwer, *Grand rounds !* and the fentry will reply, *Stand, grand rounds ! Advance ferjeant with the counterfign !* Upon which the ferjeant advances and gives the counterfign. The fentinel will then cry, *Advance, rounds !* and prefent his arms till they have paffed.

When the fentry before the guard challenges, and is anfwered, *Grand rounds !* he will reply, *Stand, grand rounds ! Turn out the guard ! Grand rounds !* Upon the fentinel's calling, the guard is to be turned out and drawn up in good or-der, with fhouldered arms, the officers taking their pofts. The officer commanding the guard will then order a ferjeant and two men to ad-vance towards the round and challenge. When the ferjeant of the guard comes within ten paces of the rounds, he is to halt and challenge brifkly. The ferjeant of the rounds is to an-fwer, *Grand rounds !* The ferjeant of the guard replies, *Stand, grand rounds ! Advance ferjeant with the counterfign !* and orders his men to pre-fent their arms. The ferjeant of the rounds

K 2   advances

advances alone, and giving the counterfign, returns to his rounds ; and the ferjeant of the guard calls to his officer, *The counterfign is right !* On which the officer of the guard calls, *Advance, rounds !* The officer of the rounds then advances alone, and on his approach the guard prefent their arms. The officer of the rounds paffes along the front of the guard immediately to the officer (who keeps his poft on the right) and gives him the parole. He then examines the guard, orders back his efcort, and demanding a new one, proceeds in the fame manner to the other guards.

A R T I C L E 6.

Honors due from Guards to General Officers and others.

To the commander in chief : All guards turn out with prefented arms ; the drums beat a march, and the officers falute.

To major generals : They turn out with prefented arms, and beat two ruffles.

To brigadier generals : They turn out with prefented arms, and beat one ruffle.

To

To officers of the day : They turn out with prefented arms, and beat according to their rank.

Except from thefe rules a general officer's guard, which turns out and pays honors only to officers of fuperior rank to the general whofe guard it is.

To colonels : Their own quarter guards turn out once a day with prefented arms ; after which they only turn out with ordered arms.

To lieutenant colonels : Their own quarter guards turn out once a day with fhouldered arms; after which they only turn out and ftand by their arms.

To majors : Their own quarter guards turn out once a day with ordered arms ; at all other times they ftand by their arms.

When a lieutenant colonel or major commands a regiment, the quarter guard is to pay him the fame honors as are ordered to a colonel.

All fentries prefent their arms to general officers, and to the field officers of their own re-

K 3   giments ;

giments ; to all other commiſſioned officers they ſtand with ſhouldered arms.

The preſident of congreſs, all governors in their own ſtates, and committees of congreſs at the army, ſhall have the ſame honors paid them as the commander in chief.

When a detachment with arms paſſes before a guard, the guard ſhall be under arms, and the drums of both beat a march.

When a detachment without arms paſſes, the guard ſhall turn out and ſtand by their arms.

After dark no honors are to be paid ; and when near the enemy, no honors are to be paid with the drum.

C H A P T E R XXIII.

Of the Arms and Ammunition, with the Methods of preſerving them.

THE preſervation of the arms and ammunition is an object that requires the greateſt attention. Commanding officers of regiments muſt be anſwerable for thoſe of their regiments, and captains for their reſpective companies. **An**

An officer of a company muſt every morning
at roll-call inſpect minutely into the ſtate of
the men's arms, accoutrements and ammunition;
and if it ſhall appear that a ſoldier has ſold, or
through careleſſneſs loſt or damaged any part
of them, he muſt be confined and puniſhed, and
ſtoppages made of his pay, as hereafter mentioned : For which purpoſe ſuch officer ſhall
certify to the commanding officer of the regiment the names of the delinquents, and the
loſſes or damages which ſhall appear of their
arms, ammunition and accoutrements ; and the
commanding officer, after due examination,
ſhall order ſtoppages to be made for whatever
ſhall appear to have been ſold, loſt or damaged
as aforeſaid. The ſtoppages to be as follows :

For a firelock, ſixteen dollars ;
    a bayonet, two dollars ;
    a ram-rod, one dollar ;
    a cartridge-box, four dollars ;
    a bayonet-belt, one dollar ;
    a ſcabbard, two thirds of a dollar ;
    a cartridge, one ſixth of a dollar ;
    a flint, one twentieth of a dollar ;
    a gun-worm, one fourth of a dollar ;
    a ſcrew-driver, one twelfth of a dollar
                          And

And for arms, accoutrements and ammunition
damaged, fuch fums as the repairs fhall coft
the ftates, to be eftimated by the brigade
conductor, or, when a corps is detached, by
fuch perfon as its commanding officer fhall
appoint for that purpofe ; provided that fuch
ftoppages do not exceed one half the delin-
quent's pay monthly.

It is highly effential to the fervice that the
ammunition fhould be at all times kept complete ; for which purpofe, as often as is neceffary, a return is to be made by each company
of the number of cartridges deficient, to the
quarter-mafter, that he may make out a general one for the regiment, to be figned by the
commanding officers of the regiment and brigade, and no time loft in fupplying the defi-
ciency. The like care is to be taken that all
deficiencies of arms and accoutrements are fupplied without lofs of time.

All arms, accoutrements and ammunition unfit for fervice, are to be carefully preferved and
fent by the commanding officer of each company to the regimental quarter-mafter, who fhall
deliver the fame to the brigade conductor, they
respectively

refpectively giving receipts for what they receive. The arms, accoutrements and ammunition of the fick and others, when delivered up, are to be taken care of in the fame manner. Before the cartridge-boxes are put in the arm-chefts, the cartridges muft be taken out, to prevent any lofs or accident.

A conductor fhall be appointed to each brigade, who fhall have under his immediate care and direction a travelling forge and five or fix armourers, an ammunition waggon, and a waggon with an arm-cheft for each battalion, each cheft to hold twenty-five arms, to receive the arms and accoutrements wanting repair, or of the men fick or abfent ; and when the arms delivered in by a battalion fhall exceed the above number, the furplus fhall be fent to the commiffary of military ftores.

The brigade conductor fhall iffue no ammunition but by order of the commanding officer of the brigade ; but may receive and deliver the arms and accoutrements of each battalion, by order of its commanding officer.

The ammunition waggon fhall contain twenty thoufand cartridges ; and in order to keep
the

the fame complete, the conductor fhall, as deficiencies arife, apply to the field commiffary, or
one of his deputies, for a fupply, or otherwife
for the neceffary materials of cartridges, and
to the major of brigade for men to make them
up under the direction of the conductor ; and
for this purpofe the brigade major fhall order
out a party of the moft careful foldiers.

The non-commiffioned officers of each company will be provided with gun-worms ; and
every day, at the noon roll-call of the company,
thofe men who have returned from duty are
to bring their arms and have their charges
drawn ; the firft ferjeant to receive the powder
and ball, and deliver the fame to the quarter-
mafter.

CHAPTER XXIV.

Of the Treatment of the Sick.

THERE is nothing which gains an officer
the love of his foldiers more than his care
of them under the diftrefs of ficknefs ; it is then
he has the power of exerting his humanity in
providing them every comfortable neceffary,
and making their fituation as agreeable as poffible.   Two

Two or three tents fhould be fet apart in every regiment for the reception of fuch fick as cannot be fent to the general hofpital, or whofe cafes may not require it. And every company fhall be conftantly furnifhed with two facks, to be filled occafionally with ftraw, and ferve as beds for the fick. Thefe facks to be provided in the fame manner as cloathing for the troops, and finally iffued by the regimental clothier to the captain of each company, who fhall be anfwerable for the fame.

When a foldier dies, or is difmiffed the hofpital, the ftraw he lay on is to be burnt, and the bedding well wafhed and aired before another is permitted to ufe it.

The ferjeants and corporals fhall every morning at roll-call give a return of the fick of their refpective fquads to the firft ferjeant, who muft make out one for the company, and lofe no time in delivering it to the furgeon, who will immediately vifit them, and order fuch as he thinks proper to the regimental hofpital; fuch whofe cafes require their being fent to the general hofpital, he is to report immediately to the furgeon general, or principal furgeon attending the army. Once

Once every week (and oftener when required) the furgeon will deliver the commanding officer of the regiment a return of the fick of the regiment, with their diforders, diftinguifhing thofe in the regimental hofpital from thofe out of it.

When a foldier is fent to the hofpital, the non-commiffioned officer of his fquad fhall deliver up his arms and accoutrements to the commanding officer of the company, that they may be depofited in the regimental arm-cheft.

When a foldier has been fick, he muft not be put on duty till he has recovered fufficient ftrength, of which the furgeon fhould be judge.

The furgeons are to remain with their regiments as well on a march as in camp, that in cafe of fudden accidents they may be at hand to apply the proper remedies.

CHAPTER XXV.
Of Reviews.

ARTICLE I.
Of Reviews of Parade.

WHEN a battalion is to be reviewed, it muft be drawn up in the following anner :
The

The ranks at four paces diftance from each other ; the colours advanced four paces from the centre ; the colonel twelve paces before the colours ; the lieutenant colonel four paces behind the colonel ; the major on the right of the battalion in the line of officers ; the adjutant behind the centre ; the officers commanding platoons eight paces before their intervals ; and the other officers on the fame line equally divided in front of their refpective platoons ; the ferjeants who covered officers take their places in the front rank of their platoons ; the other non-commiffioned officers who were in the rear, remain there, falling back four paces behind the rear rank ; and the drummers and fifers are equally divided on the wings of the battalion, dreffing with the front rank. The general officer who is to review them being within thirty paces of the battalion, the colonel orders

Battalion ! Prefent—Arms !

On which the men prefent their arms, and the drums on the right wing falute him according to his rank ; the officers and colours falute him as he paffes in front of the battalion ; and

L   on

on his arriving at the left, the drums beat the same as on the right.

The colonel then commands

Shoulder—Firelocks !

And when the general has advanced to the front,

Rear Rank ! *Clofe to the Front* !

On which the officers face to their platoons.

March !

The rear rank clofes to the front, and the officers ftepping off at the fame time, thofe commanding platoons take their pofts in the front rank, and the others go through the intervals to their pofts in the rear.

The colonel then commands

Battalion !

By Platoons ! *To the Right,—Wheel* ! *March* !

The whole wheel by platoons to the right, and march by the general ; the colonel at the head of the battalion, with the major behind him, followed by the drums of the right wing ; the adjutant on the left of the fifth platoon ; and the lieutenant colonel in the rear, preceded by the drums of the left wing.

The

The officers and colours falute when within eight paces of the general; and the colonel having faluted, advances to him.

The battalion having marched to its ground and formed, the general orders fuch exercife and manœuvres as he thinks proper.

Of Reviews of Infpection.

For a review of infpection the battalion muft not be told off into platoons, but remain in companies, at open order; the drums and fifes on the right, and the enfigns with the colours in front of their refpective companies.

The infpector begins with a general review, paffing along the front of the battalion from right to left, accompanied by the field and ftaff officers. The general review over, the colonel commands

Rear Rank ! Clofe to the Front ! March !
The rear rank clofes to the front, the officers remaining in front.

By Companies ! To the Right,—Wheel ! March !
Each company wheels to the right; the captains then open their ranks, and order

L 2   *Non-commiffioned*

*Non-commiſſioned Officers ! To the Front,—
March !*

The officers take poſt four paces, and the non-commiſſioned officers two paces, in front of their companies.

The whole then order their firelocks by word of command from their captains, except the firſt company, where the inſpection begins ; when the firſt company has been inſpected, they order their firelocks, and the next company ſhoulders ; the others proceed in the ſame manner till the whole are inſpected.

The field and ſtaff officers accompany the inſpector while he inſpects the companies ; and when the inſpection is over, the colonel forms the battalion, and cauſes it to perform any exerciſe or manœuvres the inſpector thinks proper to order.

INSTRUCTIONS.

Inſtructions for the Commandant of a Regiment.

THE ſtate having entruſted him with the care of a regiment, his greateſt ambition

ſhould

ſhould be to have it at all times and in every reſpect as complete as poſſible : To do which, he ſhould pay great attention to the following objects :

The preſervation of the ſoldiers health ſhould be his firſt and greateſt care ; and as that depends in a great meaſure on their cleanlineſs and manner of living, he muſt have a watchful eye over the officers of companies, that they pay the neceſſary attention to their men in thoſe reſpects.

The only means of keeping the ſoldiers in order is, to have them continually under the eyes of their ſuperiors ; for which reaſon the commandant ſhould uſe the utmoſt ſeverity to prevent their ſtraggling from their companies, and never ſuffer them to leave the regiment without being under the care of a non-commiſ-ſioned officer, except in caſes of neceſſity. And in order to prevent any man's being abſent from the regiment without his knowledge, he muſt often count the files, and ſee that they agree with the returns delivered him, ſtrictly obliging every man returned fit for duty to appear under arms on all occaſions ; and if any

K 3   are

are miffing, he muft oblige the commanding officer of the company to account for their abfence. In a word, the commandant ought to know upon what duty and where every man of his regiment is. To thefe points the other field officers muft alfo pay attention.

The choice of non-commiffioned officers is alfo an object of the greateft importance : the order and difcipline of a regiment depends fo much upon *their* behaviour, that too much care cannot be taken in preferring none to that truft but thofe who by their merit and good conduct are entitled to it. Honefty, fobriety, and a remarkable attention to every point of duty, with a neatnefs in their drefs, are indifpenfable requifites ; a fpirit to command refpect and obedience from the men, an expertnefs in performing every part of the exercife, and an ability to teach it, are abfolutely neceffary ; nor can a ferjeant or corporal be faid to be qualified who does not write and read in a tolerable manner.

Once every month the commandant fhould make a general infpection of his regiment, examine into the ftate of the men, their arms,

ammunition,

ammunition, accoutrements, neceffaries, camp
utenfils, and every thing belonging to the regiment, obliging the commanding officers of
companies to account ftrictly for all deficiencies.

He fhould alfo once every month affemble the
field officers and the eldeft captain, to hold a
council of adminiftration ; in which fhould be
examined the books of the feveral companies,
the pay-mafter and quarter-mafter, to fee that
all receipts and deliveries are entered in proper
order, and the affairs of the regiment duly ad-
miniftered.

All returns of the regiment being figned by
the commanding officer, he fhould examine
them with the greateft care before he fuffers
them to go out of his hands.

The commandant muft always march and encamp with his regiment ; nor muft he permit
any officer to lodge out of camp, or in a houfe,
except in cafe of ficknefs.

On a march he muft keep his regiment together as much as poffible, and not fuffer the officers to leave their platoons without his permiffion ;

miſſion ; nor permit any of them, on any pretence whatſoever, to mount on horſeback.— There is no fatigue the ſoldiers go through that the officers ſhould not ſhare ; and on all occaſions they ſhould ſet them examples of patience and perſeverance.

When a regiment is on a march, the commandant will order a ſerjeant and ſix men into the rear, to bring up all ſtragglers ; and the ſerjeant on his arrival in camp or quarters, muſt make his report to him.

In a word, the commanding officer of a regiment muſt preſerve the ſtrictteſt diſcipline and order in his corps, obliging every officer to a ſtrict performance of his duty, without relaxing in the ſmalleſt point ; puniſhing impartially the faults that are committed, without diſtinction of rank or ſervice.

Inſtructions for the Major.

THE major is particularly charged with the diſcipline, arms, accoutrements, cloathing, and generally, with the whole interior management and œconomy of the regiment.

He

He muſt have a watchful eye over the officers, and oblige them to do their duty on every occaſion ; he muſt often cauſe them to be exerciſed in his preſence, and inſtruct them how to command their platoons and preſerve their diſtances.

He muſt endeavour to make his regiment perform their exerciſe and manœuvres with the greateſt vivacity and preciſion, examine often the ſtate of the different companies, making the captains anſwer for any deficiencies he may perceive, and reporting the ſame to the colonel.

He muſt pay the greateſt attention to have all orders executed with the ſtricteſt punctuality, ſo far as reſpects his regiment ; and ſhould every week examine the adjutant's and quartermaſter's books, and ſee that all returns, orders and other matters, the objects of their reſpective duties, are regularly entered.

He muſt cauſe to be kept a regimental book, wherein ſhould be entered the name and rank of every officer, the date of his commiſſion, and the time he joined the regiment ; the name and deſcription of every non-commiſſioned officer and ſoldier, his trade or occupation, the

place

place of his birth and ufual refidence, where, when and for what term he was enlifted ; difcharges, furloughs and courts martial, copies of all returns, and every cafualty that happens in the regiment.

He muft be at all times well acquainted with the ftrength of his regiment and brigade, and the details of the army, and fee that his regiment furnifhes no more than its proportion for duty.

He muft often infpect the detachments for duty furnifhed by his regiment, fee that they are complete in every refpect, and formed agreeably to the regulations.

On a march he muft often ride along the flanks of his regiment, fee that the platoons march in order, and keep their proper diftances.

When the regiment is detached, he will poft the guards ordered by the colonel, often vifit them, examine whether the officers, non-commiffioned officers and fentinels are acquainted with their duty, and give them the neceffary inftructions.

Inftructions

Inſtruttions for the Adjutant.

THE adjutant is to be choſen from among the ſubalterns, the field officers taking care to nominate one the moſt intelligent and beſt acquainted with the ſervice.

He muſt keep an exact detail of the duty of the officers and non-commiſſioned officers of his regiment, taking care to regulate his roſter in ſuch a manner as not to have too many officers or non-commiſſioned officers of the ſame company on duty at the ſame time.

He muſt keep a book, in which he muſt every day take the general and other orders, and ſhew them to the commanding officer of the regiment, who having added thoſe he thinks neceſſary for the regiment, the adjutant muſt aſſemble the firſt ſerjeants of the companies, make them copy the orders, and give them their details for the next day.

He muſt attend the parade at the turning out of all guards or detachments, inſpect their dreſs, arms, accoutrements and ammunition, form them into platoons or ſections, and conduct them to the general or brigade parade.

When

When the regiment parades for duty or exercife, he muft count it off, and divide it into divifions and platoons, and carry the orders of the colonel where neceffary.

The adjutant is to receive no orders but from the field officers and officer commanding a battalion.

On a march he muft ride along the flanks of the regiment, to fee that regularity is obferved, and muft pay attention to the ferjeant in the rear, that he brings up all ftragglers.

On the arrival of the regiment in camp, his firft care is to form and fend off the guards ; and when the tents are pitched, he muft immediately order out the neceffary number of fatigue men to dig the vaults or finks, and open communications where neceffary. He will then form the detachments for wood, water and other neceffaries.

He muft be conftantly with the regiment, ready to receive and execute any orders that may come ; nor muft he go from his tent without leaving an officer to do his duty, or directions where he may be found.

Inftructions

Inſtructions for the Quarter-Maſter.

THE quarter-maſter, being charged with encamping and quartering the regiment, ſhould be at all times acquainted with its ſtrength, that he may require no more ground than is neceſſary, nor have more tents pitched than the number preſcribed ; for both which he is accountable.

He muſt inform the regiment where to fetch their wood, water and other neceſſaries, and where to paſture the horſes.

He muſt inſtruct the quarter-maſter ſerjeant and pioneers in the manner of laying out the camp, agreeably to the order preſcribed in the regulations.

He is anſwerable for the cleanlineſs of the camp, and that the ſoldiers make no fire any where but in the kitchens.

When the army marches, he muſt conduct the pioneers to the place appointed, and order the quarter-maſter ſerjeant to take charge of the baggage.

He is to make out all returns for camp equipage, arms, accoutrements, ammunition,

M   proviſions

proviſions and forage, and receive and diſtribute them to the regiment, taking the neceſſary vouchers for the delivery, and entering all receipts and deliveries in a book kept by him for that purpoſe.

He muſt pay particular attention to the preſervation of the camp equipage, cauſe the neceſſary repairs to be done when wanting, and return every thing unfit for uſe to the ſtores from which he drew them.

The preſervation of the arms, accoutrements and ammunition is of ſuch eſſential importance, that he muſt be ſtrictly attentive to have thoſe of the ſick, of the men on furlough, diſcharged, or detached on command without arms, taken care of and depoſited with the brigade conductor, as directed in the regulations.

Inſtructions for the Captain.

A CAPTAIN cannot be too careful of the company the ſtate has committed to his charge. He muſt pay the greateſt attention to the health of his men, their diſcipline, arms, accoutrements, ammunition, clothes and neceſſaries.

His

His firſt object ſhould be, to gain the love of his men, by treating them with every poſſible kindneſs and humanity, enquiring into their complaints, and when well founded, ſeeing them redreſſed. He ſhould know every man of his company by name and character. He ſhould often viſit thoſe who are ſick, ſpeak tenderly to them, ſee that the public proviſion, whether of medicine or diet, is duly adminiſtered, and procure them beſides ſuch comforts and conveniencies as are in his power. The attachment that ariſes from this kind of attention to the ſick and wounded, is almoſt inconceivable ; it will moreover be the means of preſerving the lives of many valuable men.

He muſt divide his company into four ſquads, placing each under the particular care of a non-commiſſioned officer, who is to be anſwerable for the dreſs and behaviour of the men of his ſquad.

He muſt be very particular in the daily and weekly inſpections of his men, cauſing all deficiencies to be immediately ſupplied; and when he diſcovers any irregularity in the dreſs or conduct of any ſoldier, he muſt not only puniſh

M 2   him

him, but the non-commiffioned officer to whofe fquad he belongs.

He muft keep a ftrict eye over the conduct of the non-commiffioned officers ; oblige them to do their duty with the greateft exactnsfs ; and ufe every poffible means to keep up a proper fubordination between them and the foldiers : For which reafon he muft never rudely reprimand them in prefence of the men, but at all times treat them with proper refpect.

He muft pay the utmoft attention to every thing which contributes to the health of the men, and oblige them to keep themfelves and every thing belonging to them in the greateft cleanlinefs and order. He muft never fuffer a man who has any infectious diforder to remain in the company, but fend him immediately to the hofpital, or other place provided for the reception of fuch patients, to prevent the fpreading of the infection. And when any man is fick, or otherwife unfit for duty, or abfent, he muft fee that his arms and accoutrements are properly taken care of, agreeably to the regulations prefcribed.

He muft keep a book, in which muft be entered

tered the name and defcription of every non-commiffioned officer and foldier of his company ; his trade or occupation ; the place of his birth and ufual refidence ; where, when and for what term he inlifted; difcharges,furloughs, copies of all returns, and every cafualty that happens in the company. He muft alfo keep an account of all arms, accoutrements, ammunition, clothing, neceffaries and camp equipage delivered his company, that on infpecting it he may be able to difcover any deficiencies.

When the company arrive at their quarters after a march, he muft not difmifs them till the guards are ordered out, and (if cantoned) the billets diftributed, which muft be as near together as poffible ; and he muft ftrictly prohibit his men from vexing the inhabitants, and caufe to be punifhed any that offend in that refpect.

He muft acquaint them with the hours of roll-call and going for provifions, with their alarm poft, and the hour of march in the morning.

If the company make any ftay in a place, he muft, previous to their marching, infpect into their condition, examine their knapfacks, and

M 3   fee

fee that they carry nothing but what is allow-
ed, it being a material object to prevent the
foldier loading himfelf with unneceffary baggage.

Inftructions for the Lieutenant.

THE lieutenant, in the abfence of the captain, commands the company, and fhould
therefore make himfelf acquainted with the
duties of that ftation ; he muft alfo be perfectly acquainted with the duties of the non-commiffioned officers and foldiers, and fee them
performed with the greateft exactnefs.

He fhould endeavour to gain the love of his
men, by his attention to every thing which
may contribute to their health and convenience. He fhould often vifit them at different
hours ; infpect into their manner of living ;
fee that their provifions are good and well
cooked, and as far as poffible oblige them to
take their meals at regulated hours. He fhould
pay attention to their complaints, and when
well founded, endeavour to get them redreffed ;
but difcourage them from complaining on every
frivolous occafion.

He

He muſt not ſuffer the ſoldiers to be ill treated by the non-commiſſioned officers through malevolence, or from any pique or reſentment; but muſt at the ſame time be careful that a proper degree of ſubordination is kept up between them.

Although no officer ſhould be ignorant of the ſervice of the guards, yet it particularly behoves the lieutenant to be perfectly acquainted with that duty ; he being oftener than any other officer entruſted with the command of a guard—a truſt of the higheſt importance, on the faithful execution of which the ſafety of an army depends; and in which the officer has frequent opportunities to diſtinguiſh himſelf by his judgment, vigilance and bravery.

Inſtructions for the Enſign.

THE enſign is in a particular manner charged with the cleanlineſs of the men, to which he muſt pay the greateſt attention.

When the company parades, and whilſt the captain and lieutenant are examining the arms and accoutrements, the enſign muſt inſpect the dreſs of the ſoldiers, obſerving whether they

are

are clean, and every thing about them in the beſt order poſſible, and duly noticing any who in theſe reſpects are deficient.

He muſt be very attentive to the conduct of the non-commiſſioned officers, obſerving that they do their duty with the greateſt exactneſs ; that they ſupport a proper authority, and at the ſame time do not ill treat the men through any pique or reſentment.

As there are only two colours to a regiment, the enſigns muſt carry them by turns, being warned for that ſervice by the adjutant. When on that duty, they ſhould conſider the importance of the truſt repoſed in them ; and when in action, reſolve not to part with the colours but with their lives. As it is by them the battalion dreſſes when marching in line, they ſhould be very careful to keep a regular ſtep, and by frequent practice accuſtom themſelves to march ſtraight forward to any given object.

Inſtructions for the Serjeant Major.

THE ſerjeant major, being at the head of the non-commiſſioned officers, muſt pay the greateſt attention to their conduct and behaviour,

our, never conniving at the leaſt irregularity committed by them or the ſoldiers, from both of whom he muſt exact the moſt implicit obedience. He ſhould be well acquainted with the interior management and diſcipline of the regiment, and the manner of keeping roſters and forming details. He muſt always attend the parade, be very expert in counting off the battalion, and in every other buſineſs of the adjutant, to whom he is an aſſiſtant.

Inſtructions for the Quarter-Maſter Serjeant.

HE is an aſſiſtant to the quarter-maſter of the regiment, and in his abſence is to do his duty, unleſs an officer be ſpecially appointed for that purpoſe : He ſhould therefore acquaint himſelf with all the duties of the quarter-maſter before mentioned. When the army marches, he muſt ſee the tents properly packed and loaded, and go with the baggage, ſee that the waggoners commit no diſorders, and that nothing is loſt out of the waggons.

Inſtructions for the Firſt Serjeant of a Company.

THE ſoldier having acquired that degree of confidence of his officers as to be appointed

ed

ed firſt ſerjeant of the company, ſhould conſider the importance of his office ; that the diſcipline of the company, the conduct of the
men, their exactneſs in obeying orders, and the
regularity of their manners, will in a great
meaſure depend on his vigilance.

He ſhould be intimately acquainted with the
character of every ſoldier of the company, and
ſhould take great pains to impreſs upon their
minds the indiſpenſable neceſſity of the ſtricteſt
obedience, as the foundation of order and regularity.

He will keep the details of the company, and
never warn a man out of his turn, unleſs particularly ordered ſo to do.

He muſt take the daily orders in a book kept
by him for that purpoſe, and ſhew them to his
officers.

He muſt every morning make a report to the
captain of the ſtate of the company, in the form
preſcribed ; and at the ſame time acquaint him
with any thing material that may have happen-
ed in the company ſince the preceding report.

He muſt parade all guards and detachments
furniſhed

furnifhed by his company, examine their arms, ammunition, accoutrements and drefs, before he carries them to the parade ; and if any man appears unfit, he muft fupply his place with another, and have the defaulter punifhed : For this purpofe he muft always warn a man or two more than ordered, to ferve as a referve, who, if not wanted, will return to their companies.

He will keep the company book (under the infpection of the captain) in which he will enter the name and defcription of every non-commiffioned officer and foldier ; his trade and occupation ; the place of his birth and ufual refidence ; where, when and for what term he was inlifted ; the bounty paid him ; the arms, ammunition, accoutrements, clothing and neceffaries delivered him, with their marks and numbers, and the times when delivered ; alfo copies of all returns, furloughs, difcharges, and every cafualty that happens in the company.

When each foldier fhall be provided with a fmall book, the firft ferjeant is to enter therein the foldier's name, a copy of his inliftment, the bounty paid him, the arms, accoutrements, clothing

clothing and neceffaries delivered him, with their marks and numbers : For this purpofe he muft be prefent at all diftributions in his company ; and as often as arms, clothing, &c. are delivered, he muft enter them in the foldier's as well as the company's book.

The firft ferjeant is not to go on any duty, unlefs with the whole company ; but is to be always in camp or quarters, to anfwer any call that may be made.

He is never to lead a platoon or fection, but is always to be a file-clofer in the formation of the company, his duty being in the company like the adjutant's in the regiment.

Inftructions for the Serjeants and Corporals.

IT being on the non-commiffioned officers that the difcipline and order of a company in a great meafure depend, they cannot be too circumfpect in their behaviour towards the men, by treating them with mildnefs, and at the fame time obliging every one to do his duty. By avoiding too great familiarity with the men, they will not only gain their love and confidence, but be treated with a proper refpect ;

fpeƈt ; whereas by a contrary conduƈt they forfeit all regard, and their authority becomes defpifed.

Each ferjeant and corporal will be in a particular manner anfwerable for the fquad committed to his care. He muft pay particular attention to their conduƈt in every refpeƈt ; that they keep themfelves and their arms always clean ; that they have their effeƈts always ready, and put where they can get them immediately, even in the dark, without confufion ; and on every fine day he muft oblige them to air their effeƈts.

When a man of his fquad is warned for duty, he muft examine him before he carries him to the parade, obliging him to take all his effeƈts with him, unlefs when fpecially ordered to the contrary.

In teaching the recruits, they muft exercife all their patience, by no means abufing them, but treating them with mildnefs, and not expeƈt too much precifion in the firft leffons, punifhing thofe only who are wilfully negligent.

They muft fupprefs all quarrels and difputes in the company ; and where other means fail, muft ufe their authority in confining the offender.

N   They

They fhould teach the foldiers of their fquads how to drefs with a foldier-like air, how to clean their arms, accoutrements, &c. and how to mount and difmount their firelocks ; for which purpofe each non-commiffioned officer fhould always be provided with a turnfcrew, and fuffer no foldier to take his arms to pieces without his permiffion.

On a march the non-commiffioned officers muft preferve order and regularity, and fuffer no man to leave the ranks without permiffion of the officer commanding the platoon.

A corporal muft teach the fentinels to challenge brifkly, and every thing elfe they are to do in their different fituations ; and when he relieves them, muft make them deliver the orders diftinctly.

When a guard is relieved, the non-commiffioned officers take the orders from thofe whom they relieve ; when fent to vifit the fentries, they fhould inftruct them in their duty. They fhould reconnoitre the roads they are to patrol in the night, that they may not lofe themfelves. They muft make their patrol with the greateft filence and attention, and where neceffary, fend

a

a faithful foldier a-head to look out. If they meet a detachment of the enemy ftronger than their own, they muft retreat in order to their own poft. In the night they muft ftop all ftrangers that approach. They muft not fuffer their men to make the leaft noife with their arms or accoutrements, and every now and then ftop and liften. On their return from patrolling, they muft report to the officer what they have feen or heard.

When a non-commiffioned officer is a file-clofer in action, he muft take care to keep the ranks and files properly clofed, and when too much crowded, make them incline from the centre. When the files of his platoon are diforderd by the lofs of men, he muft exert himfelf to drefs and complete them afrefh, with the utmoft expedition. He muft keep the greateft filence in the ranks, fee that the men load well and quick, and take good aim. He will do all in his power to encourage the foldiers, and ufe the moft vigorous means to prevent any from leaving the ranks, unlefs wounded.

Inftructions for the private Soldier.

THE recruit having received his neceffaries, fhould in the firft place learn to drefs him-

felf

felf with a foldier-like air ; to place his effects
properly in his knapfack, fo as to carry them
with eafe and convenience ; how to falute his
officers when he meets them ; to clean his arms,
wafh his linen and cook his provifions. He
fhould early accuftom himfelf to drefs in the
night ; and for that purpofe always have his
effects in his knapfack, and that placed where
he can put his hand on it in a moment, that in
cafe of alarm he may repair with the greateft
alertnefs to the parade.

When learning to march, he muft take the
greateft pains to acquire a firm ftep and a proper balance, practifing himfelf at all his leifure
hours. He muft accuftom himfelf to the greateft fteadinefs under arms, to pay attention to
the commands of his officers, and exercife himfelf continually with his firelock, in order to
acquire vivacity in his motions. He muft acquaint himfelf with the ufual beats and fignals
of the drum, and inftantly obey them.

When in the ranks, he muft always learn
the names of his right and left hand men and
file-leader, that he may be able to find his place
readily in cafe of feparation. He muft cover
his

his file-leader and drefs well in his rank, which he may be affured of doing when he can juft perceive the breaft of the third man from him. Having joined his company, he muft no longer confider himfelf as a recruit, but as a foldier ; and whenever he is ordered under arms, muft appear well dreffed, with his arms and accoutrements clean and in good order, and his knapfack, blanket, &c. ready to throw on his back in cafe he fhould be ordered to take them.

When warned for guard, he muft appear as neat as poffible, carry all his effects with him, and even when on fentry muft have them at his back. He muft receive the orders from the fentry he relieves ; and when placed before the guard-houfe, he muft inform the corporal of all that approach, and fuffer no one to enter until examined ; if he is pofted at a diftance from the guard, he will march there in order, have the orders well explained to him by the corporal, learn which is the neareft poft between him and the guard, in cafe he fhould be obliged to retire, or have any thing to communicate, and what he is to do in cafe of alarm ; or if in a town, in cafe of fire and any difturbance. He will never go more than twenty

N 3   paces

paces from his poft ; and if in a retired place, or in the night, fuffer no one to approach within ten paces of him.

A fentinel muft never reft upon his arms, but keep walking on his poft. He muft never fuffer himfelf to be relieved but by his corporal; challenge brifkly in the night, and ftop thofe who have not the counterfign ; and if any will not anfwer to the third challenge, or having been ftopped fhould attempt to efcape, he may fire on them.

When on patrol, he muft obferve the ftricteft filence, nor make the leaft noife with his arms or accoutrements.

In action he will pay the greateft attention to the commands of his officers, level well, and not throw away his fire ; take particular care to keep his rank and file, incline to that fide he dreffes to, and encourage his comrades to do their duty.

When ordered to march, he muft not charge himfelf with any unneceffary baggage ; he will march at his eafe, without however leaving his rank or file ; he fhould drink as feldom as poffible, and never ftop but when neceffity obliges
him ;

him ; in which cafe he muft afk leave of the commanding officer of the platoon.

When arrived at camp or quarters, he muft clean his arms, prepare his bed, and go for neceffaries, taking nothing without leave, nor committing any kind of excefs.

He muft always have a ftopper for the muzzle of his gun in cafe of rain, and when on a march ; at which times he will unfix his bayonet.

C O N T E N T S.

CHAP.

Explanation *of the* Plates.

APPENDIX X.

An ACT more effectually to provide for the National Defence, by establishing an Uniform Militia throughout the United States.

SEC. 1. EACH and every free able bodied white male citizen of the respective states, resident therein, who is or shall be of the age of eighteen years, and under the age of forty five years (except as is herein after excepted) shall severally and respectively be enrolled in the militia, by the Captain or commanding officer of the company, within whose bounds such citizen shall reside, and that within twelve months after the passing of this act. And it shall at all times hereafter be the duty of every such captain or commanding officer of a company, to enrol every such citizen as aforesaid, and also those who shall, from time to time, arrive at the age of 18 years, or being at the age of 18 years, and under the age of 45 years (except as before excepted) shall come to reside within his bounds ; and shall without delay notify such citizen of the said enrolment, by a proper noncommissioned officer of the company, by whom such notice may be proved. That every citizen, so enrolled and notified, shall, within six months thereafter, provide himself with a good musket or firelock, a sufficient bayonet and belt, two spare flints, and a knapsack, a pouch with a box therein to contain not less than twenty four cartridges, suited to the bore of his musket or firelock, each cartridge to contain a proper quantity of powder and ball ; or with a good rifle, knapsack, shot pouch, and powder horn, twenty balls suited to the bore of his rifle, and a quarter of a pound of powder ; and shall appear so armed, accoutred and provided, when called out to exercise or into service, except, that when called out on company days to exercise only, he may appear without a knapsack. That the commissioned officers shall severally be armed with a sword or hanger, and espontoon ; and that from and after five years from the passing of this act, all muskets for arming the militia as is herein required, shall be of bores sufficient for balls of the eighteenth part of a pound ; and every citizen so enrolled,

rolled, and providing himself with the arms, ammunition and accoutrements required as aforesaid, shall hold the same exempted from all suits, distresses, executions or sales, for debt or for the payment of taxes.

SEC. 2. *And be it further enacted*, That the Vice President of the United States; the officers, judicial and executive, of the government of the United States; the members of both houses of Congress, and their respective officers; all custom house officers, with their clerks; all post officers, and stagedrivers who are employed in the care and conveyance of the mail of the post office of the United States; all ferrymen employed at any ferry on the post road; all inspectors of exports; all pilots; all mariners actually employed in the sea service of any citizen or merchant within the United States; and all persons who now are or may be hereafter exempted by the laws of the respective states, shall be and are hereby exempted from militia duty, notwithstanding their being above the age of eighteen and under the age of forty five years.

SEC. 3. *And be it further enacted*, That within one year after the passing of this act, the militia of the respective states shall be arranged into divisions, brigades, regiments, battalions, and companies, as the legislature of each state shall direct; and each division, brigade, and regiment, shall be numbered at the formation thereof; and a record made of such numbers in the adjutant general's office in the state; and when in the field, or in service in the state, each division, brigade, and regiment shall, respectively, take rank according to their numbers, reckoning the first or lowest number highest in rank. That if the same be convenient, each brigade shall consist of four regiments; each regiment of two battalions; each battalion of five companies; each company of sixty four privates. That the said militia shall be officered by the respective states, as follows: To each division one major general with two aids de camp, with the rank of major; to each brigade, one brigadier general with one brigade inspector, to serve also as a brigade major, with the rank of a major; to each regiment, one lieutenant colonel commandant; and to each battalion, one major; to each company, one captain, one lieutenant, one ensign, four serjeants, four corporals, one drummer, and one fifer or bugler. That there shall be a regimental staff, to consist of one adjutant, and one quartermaster, to rank as lieutenants; one paymaster; one surgeon, and one surgeon's mate; one serjeant major; one drum major, and one fife major.

SEC.

SEC. 4. *And be it further enacted*, That out of the militia enrolled as is herein directed, there shall be formed for
each battalion, at least one company of grenadiers, light infantry or riflemen ; and that to each division there shall be,
at least, one company of artillery, and one troop of horse :
There shall be to each company of artillery, one captain, two
lieutenants, four serjeants, four corporals, six gunners, six
bombardiers, one drummer, and one fifer. The officers to
be armed with a sword or hanger, a fuzee, bayonet and belt,
with a cartridge box to contain twelve cartridges ; and each
private or matrofs shall furnish himself with all the equip-
ments of a private in the infantry, until proper ordnance and
field artillery is provided. There shall be to each troop of
horse, one captain, two lieutenants, one cornet, four serjeants, four corporals, one saddler, one farrier, and one trum-
peter. The commissioned officers to furnish themselves with
good horses, of at least fourteen hands and an half high, and
to be armed with a sword and pair of pistols, the holsters of
which to be covered with bear skin caps. Each dragoon to
furnish himself with a serviceable horse, at least fourteen hands
and an half high, a good saddle, bridle, mailpillion and valife,
holsters, and a breast plate and crupper, a pair of boots and
spurs ; a pair of pistols, a sabre, and a cartouch box to contain twelve cartridges for pistols. That each company of
artillery and troop of horse shall be formed of volunteers from
the brigade, at the discretion of the commander in chief of
the state, not exceeding one company of each to a regiment,
nor more in number than one eleventh part of the infantry,
and shall be uniformly clothed in regimentals, to be furnished
at their own expense ; the colour and fashion to be determined by the brigadier commanding the brigade to which they
belong.

SEC. 5. *And be it further enacted*, That each battalion
and regiment shall be provided with the state and regimental
colours by the field officers, and each company with a drum
and fife or bugle horn, by the commissioned officers of the
company, in such manner as the legislature of the respective
states shall direct.

SEC. 6. *And be it further enacted*, That there shall be
an adjutant general appointed in each state, whose duty it
shall be to distribute all orders from the commander in chief
of the state to the several corps ; to attend all publick reviews,
when the commander in chief of the state shall review the
militia, or any part thereof ; to obey all orders from him relative to carrying into execution, and perfecting, the system
of

of military difcipline eftablifhed by this act ; to furnifh blank forms of different returns that may be required ; and to explain the principles on which they fhould be made ; to receive from the feveral officers of the different corps throughout the ftate, returns of the militia under their command, reporting the actual fituation of their arms, accoutrements, and ammunition, their delinquencies, and every other thing which relates to the general advancement of good order and difcipline : All which, the feveral officers of the divifions, brigades, regiments, and battalions are hereby required to make in the ufual manner, fo that the faid adjutant general may be duly furnifhed therewith : From all which returns he fhall make proper abftracts, and lay the fame annually before the commander in chief of the ftate.

Sec. 7. *And be it further enacted,* That the rules of difcipline, approved and eftablifhed by Congrefs, in their refolution of the twenty ninth of March, 1779, fhall be the rules of difcipline to be obferved by the militia throughout the United States, except fuch deviations from the faid rules, as may be rendered neceffary by the requifitions of this act, or by fome other unavoidable circumftances. It fhall be the duty of the commanding officer at every mufter, whether by battalion, regiment or fingle company, to caufe the militia to be exercifed and trained, agreeably to the faid rules of difcipline.

Sec. 8. *And be it further enacted,* That all commiffioned officers fhall take rank according to the date of their commiffions ; and when two of the fame grade bear an equal date, then their rank to be determined by lots, to be drawn by them before the commanding officer of the brigade, regiment, battalion, company or detachment.

Sec. 9. *And be it further enacted,* That if any perfon, whether officer or foldier, belonging to the militia of any ftate, and called out into the fervice of the United States, be wounded or difabled while in actual fervice, he fhall be taken care of and provided for at the publick expenfe.

Sec. 10. *And be it further enacted,* That it fhall be the duty of the brigade infpector, to attend the regimental and battalion meetings of the militia compofing their feveral brigades, during the time of their being under arms, to infpect their arms, ammunition and accoutrements ; fuperintend their exercife and manœuvres, and introduce the fyftem of military difcipline before defcribed, throughout the brigade, agreeable to law, and fuch orders as they fhall, from time to time receive

UNITED STATES MILITIA ACT.

ceive from the commander in chief of the ſtate; to make returns to the adjutant general of the ſtate, at leaſt once in every year, of the militia of the brigade to which he belongs, reporting therein the actual ſituation of the arms, accoutrements
and ammunition of the ſeveral corps, and every other thing
which, in his judgment, may relate to their government and
the general advancement of good order and military diſcipline; and the adjutant general ſhall make a return of all the
militia of the ſtate, to the commander in chief of the ſaid
ſtate, and a duplicate of the ſame to the Preſident of the United States.

And whereas ſundry corps of artillery, cavalry and infantry, now exiſt in ſeveral of the ſaid ſtates, which by the laws,
cuſtoms, or uſages thereof, have not been incorporated with,
or ſubject to the general regulations of the militia:

SEC. 11. *Be it enacted,* That ſuch corps retain their accuſtomed privileges, ſubject, neverthelefs, to all other duties
required by this act, in like manner with the other militia.

Approved, May 8th, 1792.

GEORGE WASHINGTON,

PRESIDENT *of the* UNITED STATES.

A CATALOG OF SELECTED
DOVER BOOKS
IN ALL FIELDS OF INTEREST

A CATALOG OF SELECTED DOVER
BOOKS IN ALL FIELDS OF INTEREST

DRAWINGS OF REMBRANDT, edited by Seymour Slive. Updated Lippmann, Hofstede de Groot edition, with definitive scholarly apparatus. All portraits, biblical sketches, landscapes, nudes. Oriental figures, classical studies, together with selection of work by followers. 550 illustrations. Total of 630pp. 9⅛ × 12¼.
21485-0, 21486-9 Pa., Two-vol. set $29.90

GHOST AND HORROR STORIES OF AMBROSE BIERCE, Ambrose Bierce. 24 tales vividly imagined, strangely prophetic, and decades ahead of their time in technical skill: "The Damned Thing," "An Inhabitant of Carcosa," "The Eyes of the Panther," "Moxon's Master," and 20 more. 199pp. 5⅜ × 8½. 20767-6 Pa. $3.95

ETHICAL WRITINGS OF MAIMONIDES, Maimonides. Most significant ethical works of great medieval sage, newly translated for utmost precision, readability. Laws Concerning Character Traits, Eight Chapters, more. 192pp. 5⅜ × 8½.
24522-5 Pa. $4.50

THE EXPLORATION OF THE COLORADO RIVER AND ITS CANYONS, J. W. Powell. Full text of Powell's 1,000-mile expedition down the fabled Colorado in 1869. Superb account of terrain, geology, vegetation, Indians, famine, mutiny, treacherous rapids, mighty canyons, during exploration of last unknown part of continental U.S. 400pp. 5⅜ × 8½. 20094-9 Pa. $7.95

HISTORY OF PHILOSOPHY, Julián Marías. Clearest one-volume history on the market. Every major philosopher and dozens of others, to Existentialism and later. 505pp. 5⅜ × 8½. 21739-6 Pa. $9.95

ALL ABOUT LIGHTNING, Martin A. Uman. Highly readable non-technical survey of nature and causes of lightning, thunderstorms, ball lightning, St. Elmo's Fire, much more. Illustrated. 192pp. 5⅜ × 8½. 25237-X Pa. $5.95

SAILING ALONE AROUND THE WORLD, Captain Joshua Slocum. First man to sail around the world, alone, in small boat. One of great feats of seamanship told in delightful manner. 67 illustrations. 294pp. 5⅜ × 8½. 20326-3 Pa. $4.95

LETTERS AND NOTES ON THE MANNERS, CUSTOMS AND CONDI-TIONS OF THE NORTH AMERICAN INDIANS, George Catlin. Classic account of life among Plains Indians: ceremonies, hunt, warfare, etc. 312 plates. 572pp. of text. 6⅛ × 9¼. 22118-0, 22119-9, Pa. Two-vol. set $17.90

ALASKA: The Harriman Expedition, 1899, John Burroughs, John Muir, et al. Informative, engrossing accounts of two-month, 9,000-mile expedition. Native peoples, wildlife, forests, geography, salmon industry, glaciers, more. Profusely illustrated. 240 black-and-white line drawings. 124 black-and-white photographs. 3 maps. Index. 576pp. 5⅜ × 8½. 25109-8 Pa. $11.95

AMERICAN CLIPPER SHIPS: 1833–1858, Octavius T. Howe & Frederick C. Matthews. Fully-illustrated, encyclopedic review of 352 clipper ships from the period of America's greatest maritime supremacy. Introduction. 109 halftones. 5 black-and-white line illustrations. Index. Total of 928pp. 5⅜ × 8½.
25115-2, 25116-0 Pa., Two-vol. set $17.90

TOWARDS A NEW ARCHITECTURE, Le Corbusier. Pioneering manifesto by great architect, near legendary founder of "International School." Technical and aesthetic theories, views on industry, economics, relation of form to function, "mass-production spirit," much more. Profusely illustrated. Unabridged translation of 13th French edition. Introduction by Frederick Etchells. 320pp. 6⅛ × 9¼. (Available in U.S. only)
25023-7 Pa. $8.95

THE BOOK OF KELLS, edited by Blanche Cirker. Inexpensive collection of 32 full-color, full-page plates from the greatest illuminated manuscript of the Middle Ages, painstakingly reproduced from rare facsimile edition. Publisher's Note. Captions. 32pp. 9⅜ × 12¼.
24345-1 Pa. $4.95

BEST SCIENCE FICTION STORIES OF H. G. WELLS, H. G. Wells. Full novel *The Invisible Man*, plus 17 short stories: "The Crystal Egg," "Aepyornis Island," "The Strange Orchid," etc. 303pp. 5⅜ × 8½. (Available in U.S. only)
21531-8 Pa. $6.95

AMERICAN SAILING SHIPS: Their Plans and History, Charles G. Davis. Photos, construction details of schooners, frigates, clippers, other sailcraft of 18th to early 20th centuries—plus entertaining discourse on design, rigging, nautical lore, much more. 137 black-and-white illustrations. 240pp. 6⅛ × 9¼.
24658-2 Pa. $6.95

ENTERTAINING MATHEMATICAL PUZZLES, Martin Gardner. Selection of author's favorite conundrums involving arithmetic, money, speed, etc., with lively commentary. Complete solutions. 112pp. 5⅜ × 8½.
25211-6 Pa. $2.95

THE WILL TO BELIEVE, HUMAN IMMORTALITY, William James. Two books bound together. Effect of irrational on logical, and arguments for human immortality. 402pp. 5⅜ × 8½.
20291-7 Pa. $7.95

THE HAUNTED MONASTERY and THE CHINESE MAZE MURDERS, Robert Van Gulik. 2 full novels by Van Gulik continue adventures of Judge Dee and his companions. An evil Taoist monastery, seemingly supernatural events; overgrown topiary maze that hides strange crimes. Set in 7th-century China. 27 illustrations. 328pp. 5⅜ × 8½.
23502-5 Pa. $6.95

CELEBRATED CASES OF JUDGE DEE (DEE GOONG AN), translated by Robert Van Gulik. Authentic 18th-century Chinese detective novel; Dee and associates solve three interlocked cases. Led to Van Gulik's own stories with same characters. Extensive introduction. 9 illustrations. 237pp. 5⅜ × 8½.
23337-5 Pa. $4.95

Prices subject to change without notice.
Available at your book dealer or write for free catalog to Dept. GI, Dover Publications, Inc., 31 East 2nd St., Mineola, N.Y. 11501. Dover publishes more than 175 books each year on science, elementary and advanced mathematics, biology, music, art, literary history, social sciences and other areas.